KNOW YOUR BIBLE

ACTIVITY BOOK for Kids

YOU are the reason we do what we do here at Barbour Publishing. We promise that we will always use our God-given talents to produce content with you in mind—and that we will remain biblically faithful, no matter what.

Thank you for being the heart of our business.

Editorial assistance by Jennifer Hahn. Artwork by Kathy Arbuckle and Ken Save.

ISBN 979-8-89151-277-1

Published by Barbour Publishing, Inc., 1810 Barbour Drive, Uhrichsville, Ohio 44683, www.barbourbooks.com

Our mission is to inspire the world with the life-changing message of the Bible.

Printed in the United States of America.

KNOW YOUR BIBLE ACTIVITY BOOK FOR KIDS

This book is jam-packed with Bible-based pencil-and-paper games. You'll have fun as you learn more about God's Word!

Here are more than 100 crosswords, word searches, secret codes, fill-in-the-blanks, and picture fun pages. They cover many of the mostt important stories and ideas of scripture. And they're all designed to help you know your Bible better.

Here's what to do with each kind of puzzle:

- ***Crosswords:*** Fill in the puzzle grid by answering the "across" and "down" clues. If you need help, you can look up the verse references in the Bible.
- ***Word searches:*** In the puzzle grid, find and circle the **bolded** search words in the scripture. The search words might run forward, backward, up, down, or on the diagonal.
- ***Decoders:*** For every two-digit number in the puzzle, find the correct letter in the decoder grid. The first number is the row (the numbers running down the left side of the grid). The second number is the column (the numbers running across the top of the grid). After you've figured out all the letters and put them in the puzzle, they'll spell out an important Bible verse.
- ***Acrostics:*** Read the definition in the left-hand column. Write the correct word in the right-hand column. Then place the coded letters from the right-hand column into the puzzle below. It will spell out a great Bible verse.
- ***Picture fun:*** Solve a maze, connect the dots, finish the picture. . .and color them all!

Looking for something fun and worthwhile to do? You're going to love *Know Your Bible Activity Book for Kids*!

Note:

Scripture quotations marked KJV are taken from the King James Version of the Bible.
Scriptures marked NLV are taken from the New Life Version,
while verses marked SKJV are from the Barbour Simplified KJV Bible.
You can find the first two online at **BibleGateway.com**;
the third is available at **simplifiedkjv.com.**

THE BIBLE IS ALL ABOUT JESUS!

Jesus kept on telling them what Moses and all the early preachers had said about Him in the Holy Writings.

LUKE 24:27 NLV

The Bible is much more than just a book. The Bible is the perfect Word of God! It teaches us how to think and behave so that we can become more like God. And we really know what God is like by getting to know His Son, Jesus Christ.

1. WHERE THE BIBLE COMES FROM, AND WHAT IT DOES — WORD SEARCH

All the **Holy Writings** are God-given and are made **alive** by Him. Man is helped when he is **taught** God's **Word**. It **shows** what is **wrong**. It **changes** the way of a man's life. It shows him how to be **right** with God. It gives the man who **belongs** to **God** everything he needs to **work** well for Him.

2 Timothy 3:16–17 NLV

S	K	R	O	W	D	R	S	K	Y
R	E	T	T	O	N	G	F	W	L
T	L	G	G	A	N	T	S	O	O
H	M	B	N	I	U	H	N	R	H
G	T	Q	T	A	O	G	D	D	C
I	P	I	K	W	H	V	H	M	B
R	R	Z	S	L	H	C	C	T	Z
W	T	A	L	I	V	E	Y	P	K
M	T	M	S	G	N	O	L	E	B
Z	K	P	G	N	O	R	W	F	T

2. NAMES FOR THE BIBLE, FROM THE BIBLE — CROSSWORD

All Quotations SKJV

Across

1 "____ of the Lord" (Psalm 1:2)

4 "word of the ____" (1 Peter 1:25)

5 "____ of Christ" (Romans 1:16)

9 "____ of the law" (Deuteronomy 31:26)

10 "word of ____" (Colossians 3:16)

Down

1 "____ words" (Acts 7:38)

2 "____ of life" (Philippians 2:16)

3 "____ of the book" (Psalm 40:7)

6 "____ of the Spirit" (Ephesians 6:17)

7 "____ to my path" (Psalm 119:105)

8 "every word that proceeds from the ____ of God" (Matthew 4:4)

GOD SPOKE HIS WORD TO MEN, WHO WROTE IT DOWN FOR US

No part of the Holy Writings came long ago because of what man wanted to write. But holy men who belonged to God spoke what the Holy Spirit told them.

2 Peter 1:21 NLV

The Bible teaches us everything God wants us to know. And the biggest truth is that He loves us and wants us to be part of His family!

3. WHY WE HAVE THE BIBLE — DECODER

54 42-41-53-22 51-45-54-32-32-22-25 32-42-22-43-22 32-42-54-25-34-43 32-13 14-13-12 51-42-13 23-22-33-54-22-53-22 54-25 32-42-22 25-41-15-22 13-44 32-42-22 43-13-25 13-44 34-13-21, 32-42-41-32 14-13-12 15-41-14 31-25-13-51 32-42-41-32 14-13-12 42-41-53-22 22-32-22-45-25-41-33 33-54-44-22, 41-25-21 32-42-41-32 14-13-12 15-41-14 23-22-33-54-22-53-22 54-25 32-42-22 25-41-15-22 13-44 32-42-22 43-13-25 13-44 34-13-21.

1 John 5:13 SKJV

	1	2	3	4	5
1	C	U	O	Y	M
2	D	E	B	P	N
3	K	T	L	G	X
4	A	H	S	F	R
5	W	Q	V	I	J

4. WHAT THE BIBLE DOES — ACROSTIC

First book of the New Testament	8-27-43-32-23-5-39
Bible book before Titus	20-47-1-17-35-11-46
Book of the Bible with the shortest name	50-9-16
Second-to-last book of the New Testament	2-14-52-3
Longest book of the Bible	48-18-31-26-53-42
The 22nd book in the Bible	12-25-40-4 38-21 56-15-36-49-6-29-57
Last book of the New Testament	41-7-34-22-13-37-28-55-44-19
Last book of the Old Testament	33-51-10-30-24-45-54

21-44-41 43-23-5 39-9-41-52 44-21 4-17-52 54-18 13-47-34-55-19-4 27-40-52 48-44-39-3-41-21-14-26 31-57-52 42-45-31-41-48-5-41 32-23-37-19 51-19-46 28-39-17 – 3-52-4-22-52 18-39-44-41-52, 48-54-7-41-24-47-40-4 22-34-5-57 43-9 32-45-3 52-55-34-54-52-47-19-4 44-21 42-9-14-10 30-19-52 12-48-55-41-54-28, 27-40-52 44-21 43-23-22 2-17-47-57-32-56 31-19-52 53-37-41-41-44-39, 51-57-52 55-18 30 52-54-42-24-3-41-40-7-41 9-21 43-45-22 43-23-44-14-4-45-32-18 27-57-52 47-19-28-5-57-43-55-9-40-42 44-21 32-23-7 45-7-31-41-32.

Hebrews 4:12 SKJV

BIBLE WRITERS INCLUDED KINGS, SHEPHERDS, PROPHETS, AND FOLLOWERS OF JESUS, LIKE JOHN

But these are written so you may believe that Jesus is the Christ, the Son of God. When you put your trust in Him, you will have life that lasts forever through His name.

JOHN 20:31 NLV

The Bible is really all about Jesus. He is God's only Son and the Savior of the world. Jesus came to earth to show God's love for all people.

5. HOW THE BIBLE DESCRIBES JESUS — CROSSWORD

All Quotations SKJV

Across

3 "____ of God" (John 1:29)

4 "____ and Omega" (Revelation 1:8)

5 "Apostle and High ____" (Hebrews 3:1)

7 "the true ____" (John 15:1)

8 "____ of kings" (1 Timothy 6:15)

9 "Lord of ____" (1 Timothy 6:15)

Down

1 "____ of life" (John 6:35)

2 "the good ____" (John 10:11)

3 "the way, the truth, and the ____" (John 14:6)

6 "beloved ____" (Luke 9:35)

6. WHO JESUS IS — WORD SEARCH

W	T	C	K	E	B	N	A	M	E
R	R	S	F	Y	O	C	N	B	B
E	K	I	I	C	O	V	L	E	T
V	L	Y	T	R	K	M	L	G	T
E	G	Y	Q	T	H	I	R	R	S
R	J	N	Q	W	E	C	G	K	U
O	L	A	L	V	R	N	R	Z	R
F	L	M	E	N	D	O	D	Y	T
F	O	L	L	O	W	E	R	S	H
S	U	S	E	J	K	Y	K	M	F

Jesus did **many** other powerful **works** in front of His **followers**. They are not **written** in this book. But these are written so you may believe that **Jesus** is the **Christ**, the Son of God. When you put your **trust** in Him, you will have **life** that lasts **forever** through His **name**.
JOHN 20:30–31 NLV

THE BIBLE'S BOOK OF GENESIS: GOD CREATES A WORLD

And God made man in His own likeness. In the likeness of God He made him. He made both male and female.

GENESIS 1:27 NLV

The Bible's first book never says where God came from. Genesis just starts with Him: "In the beginning God. . . ." Chapters 1 and 2 show how God made the universe and everything in it just by speaking: "God said. . .and it was so" (1:9, 11, 14–15). But humans got special attention from God. He "formed man of the dust of the ground, and breathed into his nostrils the breath of life" (2:7). Then God made a woman, Eve, from a rib of the man, Adam!

7. IN THE BEGINNING, GOD. . . — DECODER

. . .13-22-52-54 24-41-21-13 45-21-23-25-42-45-53 23-25-54 25-54-22-44-54-45-35 22-45-52 23-25-54 54-22-41-23-25. 23-25-54 54-22-41-23-25 11-22-35 22-45 54-13-43-23-34 11-22-35-23-54 22-45-52 52-22-41-31-45-54-35-35 11-22-35 21-44-54-41 23-25-54 52-54-54-43 11-22-23-54-41-35. 22-45-52 23-25-54 35-43-42-41-42-23 21-24 53-21-52 11-22-35 13-21-44-42-45-53 21-44-54-41 23-25-54 23-21-43 21-24 23-25-54 11-22-23-54-41-35.

Genesis 1:1–2 NLV

	1	2	3	4	5
1	W	Q	M	U	J
2	O	A	T	F	H
3	K	B	L	Y	S
4	R	I	P	V	N
5	C	D	G	E	X

8. ADAM, EVE, AND EDEN — CROSSWORD

All Quotations SKJV

Across

2 ". . .man became a _____ soul" (Genesis 2:7)

5 The man was not to eat from the tree of the knowledge of good and ____ (Genesis 2:16–17)

8 "It is not good that man should be ____" (Genesis 2:18)

9 ". . .the Lord God caused a deep ____ to fall on Adam" (Genesis 2:21)

Down

1 God used a ____ from Adam to create the woman (Genesis 2:22)

3 Adam gave each living creature a ____ (Genesis 2:19)

4 The tree of ____ was in the middle of the garden (Genesis 2:9)

6 What Adam was supposed to do for the garden of Eden (Genesis 2:15)

7 "And the Lord God formed man from the ____ of the ground. . . ." (Genesis 2:7)

THE BIBLE'S BOOK OF GENESIS: ADAM AND EVE BRING SIN INTO THE WORLD

So the Lord God sent him out from the garden of Eden, to work the ground from which he was taken. So He drove the man out. And He placed cherubim east of the garden of Eden with a sword of fire that turned every way. They kept watch over the path to the tree of life.

GENESIS 3:23–24 NLV

The first two people on earth were Adam and Eve. They lived in a perfect place and walked and talked with God. But Adam and Eve ruined things by disobeying God. A talking serpent—the devil—tempted them to sin. Sin is a destroyer. Soon, the world's first child—Cain—murdered his own brother, Abel.

9. ADAM AND EVE'S SIN — WORD SEARCH

And when the **woman** saw that the **tree** was good for **food**, and that it was **pleasant** to the **eyes**, and a tree to be **desired** to make one **wise**, she **took** some of its **fruit** and ate, and **gave** also to her **husband** with her, and he **ate**.
GENESIS 3:6 SKJV

N	R	X	E	S	I	W	N	M	E
P	L	C	R	N	E	K	G	V	D
N	L	A	T	E	Y	Q	A	N	V
T	T	E	K	K	E	G	A	J	D
I	J	L	A	M	S	B	C	E	X
U	K	N	D	S	S	K	S	K	E
R	Y	A	K	U	A	I	T	E	L
F	K	M	H	O	R	N	R	F	N
F	O	O	D	E	O	T	T	R	C
C	G	W	D	G	M	T	N	R	T

10. CAIN AND ABEL — ACROSTIC

All Quotations SKJV

What Eve did before she gave birth to Cain (Genesis 4:1) 11-26-4-20-5-29-38-43-1

Eve said, "I have gotten a ___ from the LORD" (Genesis 4:1) 27-24-13

Abel was Cain's ______ (Genesis 4:2) 21-30-10-3-31-28-16

Animal that Abel kept (Genesis 4:2) 8-18-9-19-25

What Cain grew (Genesis 4:3) 34-7-23-17-14

How Cain felt when God rejected his offering (Genesis 4:5) 2-39-37-42-40

"If you do ___, shall you not be accepted?" (Genesis 4:7) 41-32-6-33

What Cain did with Abel before he slew him (Genesis 4:8) 22-36-12-35-15-44

24-13-1 3-18-43 12-26-7-44 8-2-17-44 14-10 11-36-29-4, "41-31-5-16-15 29-8 2-21-28-33 40-10-23-30 21-42-10-22-31-9-16?" 36-39-1 18-43 8-24-17-1, "29 44-26 4-10-22 35-39-10-41. 24-27 29 27-40 21-7-26-3-18-5-16 ' 8 35-5-9-25-32-30?" 36-13-44 31-32 8-2-17-1, "41-31-2-14 18-24-38-9 40-10-23 44-26-39-32? 14-18-5 38-26-17-20-5 10-34 40-10-23-7 21-7-26-22-31-19-42 ' 8 21-33-26-10-1 11-30-29-43-8 3-10 27-5 34-16-26-27 22-31-28 37-42-26-23-4-44."

GENESIS 4:9–10 SKJV

THE BIBLE'S BOOK OF GENESIS: NOAH BUILDS THE ARK

Then God said to Noah, "I have decided to make an end to all the people on the earth. They are the cause of very much trouble. See, I will destroy them as I destroy the earth. Make a large boat of gopher wood for yourself.

Genesis 6:13–14 NLV

Sin got worse and worse in the world. People were so bad that God was sad and angry. He decided to flood the whole earth! God chose a good man named Noah to be saved. Noah and his family would build an ark (a big boat). They would escape the flood along with a bunch of animals on the ark. They took a male and a female of every kind of animal on earth!

11. NOAH'S ARK — CROSSWORD

All Quotations SKJV

Across

4 The kind of wood to be used to build the ark (Genesis 6:14)

5 "But Noah found ____ in the eyes of the LORD" (Genesis 6:8)

8 The ark's height was ____ cubits (Genesis 6:15)

Down

1 Noah had three sons: Shem, Ham, and ____ (Genesis 6:10)

2 Two of every ____ of animal was to go into the ark (Genesis 6:19)

3 The flood waters continued for ____ days (Genesis 7:17)

6 What Noah built to the Lord after the flood (Genesis 8:20)

7 The ark's width was ____ cubits (Genesis 6:15)

9 The ark's length was ____ hundred cubits (Genesis 6:15)

12. THE RAINBOW — DECODER

	1	2	3	4	5
1	B	I	X	F	O
2	M	S	A	W	J
3	G	V	H	D	U
4	R	K	P	Y	L
5	C	Z	N	T	E

"24-33-55-53 12 11-41-12-53-31 51-45-15-35-34-22 15-32-55-41 54-33-55 55-23-41-54-33 23-53-34 54-33-55 41-23-12-53 – 11-15-24 12-22 22-55-55-53 12-53 54-33-55 51-45-15-35-34-22, 12 24-12-45-45 41-55-21-55-21-11-55-41 21-44 23-31-41-55-55-21-55-53-54 54-33-23-54 12-22 11-55-54-24-55-55-53 21-55 23-53-34 44-15-35 23-53-34 55-32-55-41-44 45-12-32-12-53-31 54-33-12-53-31 15-14 23-45-45 14-45-55-22-33. 53-55-32-55-41 23-31-23-12-53 24-12-45-45 54-33-55 24-23-54-55-41 11-55-51-15-21-55 23 14-45-15-15-34 54-15 34-55-22-54-41-15-44 23-45-45 14-45-55-22-33."

GENESIS 9:14–15 NLV

THE BIBLE'S BOOK OF GENESIS: GOD MAKES A PROMISE TO ABRAHAM AND SARAH

When Abram was ninety-nine years old, the Lord came to him and said, "I am God All-powerful. Obey Me, and be without blame. And I will keep My agreement between Me and you. I will give you many children."

Genesis 17:1–2 NLV

Noah's sons and their wives started families after the flood. After many years, the earth was full of people again. From all of them, God chose a man named Abraham. He would start a special nation to be called "Israel." It was a wonderful promise. But Abraham didn't have even one child—yet. God would give him and his wife, Sarah, a miracle baby named Isaac. God's promise would take time. But Isaac would have a son named Jacob, and Jacob would have twelve sons. They started the "twelve tribes of Israel," and God promised to give them a special land called Canaan.

13. ABRAHAM AND SARAH — ACROSTIC

All Quotations SKJV

God told Abraham to _____ before him (Genesis 17:1)	28-10-31-4
What God made with Abraham (Genesis 17:2)	33-22-1-25-11-18-2-14
God said Abraham would be the "_____ of many nations" (Genesis 17:4)	30-5-19-23-27-12
Abraham's name before God changed it (Genesis 17:5)	24-16-29-8-17
What Abraham did when he was told he would have a son (Genesis 17:17)	9-7-32-13-20-3-34
Abraham and Sarah's son's name (Genesis 21:3)	15-26-35-6-21

10-11-34 7-16-12-35-23-5-17 33-8-9-31-25-34 19-20-27 11-10-17-3 22-30 23-15-26 26-22-2 28-23-22 28-5-26

16-22-29-11 19-22 23-15-17, 28-23-17 26-10-29-24-20 16-22-29-27 19-22 23-15-17, 15-26-10-18-33.

GENESIS 21:3 SKJV

14. ISAAC'S TWIN SONS — WORD SEARCH

Abraham was the father of Isaac. **Isaac** was forty years old when he married **Rebekah**. . . . Isaac prayed to the **Lord** for his wife, because she could not give birth and the Lord **answered** him. Rebekah was able to give birth. But the **babies** within her fought together. . . . The Lord said to her, "Two **nations** are within you. Two peoples will be divided from your body. One will be **stronger** than the other. And the older will serve the **younger**." When the day came for her to give birth, there were two babies to be born. The first to come out was **red** and he had **hair** all over his body. They gave him the name of **Esau**. Then the brother was born. His hand was **holding** Esau's heel. So he was given the name of **Jacob**.

GENESIS 25:19–26 NLV

```
N M R E G N U O Y A
S N O I T A N N C N
S M M R Y R Q A Y S
T G M I G L A D B W
R N A A B S O A E E
O I H H I O B R P R
N D A P H I C U D E
G L R M E L A A K D
E O B S F S T Y J T
R H A R E B E K A H
```

THE BIBLE'S BOOK OF GENESIS: MEET JOSEPH, THE SON OF JACOB (ALSO CALLED ISRAEL)

Now Israel loved Joseph more than all his sons, because Joseph was born when he was an old man. And Israel made him a long coat of many colors.

Genesis 37:3 NLV

Joseph had ten older brothers—and they all hated him. They were jealous because Joseph was their dad's favorite. He even wore a special coat that Jacob made for him. The older brothers got so mad that they wanted to kill Joseph. But in the end, they decided to sell him to traveling merchants. He was carried off to Egypt as a slave.

15. YOUNG JOSEPH — CROSSWORD

All Quotations SKJV

Across

1 Joseph's brothers dipped his special coat in a goat's _____ (Genesis 37:32)

5 Joseph's father, also known as Jacob, who gave him a special coat (Genesis 37:3)

7 What Joseph was thrown into (Genesis 37:22)

8 Which of Joseph's brother didn't want to hurt him? (Genesis 37:21)

Down

2 Joseph's brothers hated him because of a _____ he had (Genesis 37:5)

3 Joseph asked a man where his brothers were feeding these (Genesis 37:15–16)

4 Jacob tore his _____ when he thought his favorite son had died (Genesis 37:33–34)

6 A place where Joseph looked for his brothers (Genesis 37:14)

16. SOLD AS A SLAVE! — DECODER

	1	2	3	4	5
1	K	C	Y	Q	M
2	G	O	E	X	S
3	T	B	V	I	D
4	N	J	P	L	W
5	F	U	H	R	A

25-22-15-23 15-34-35-34-55-41-34-31-23 31-54-55-35-23-54-25 45-23-54-23 43-55-25-25-34-41-21 32-13. 25-22 31-53-23 32-54-22-31-53-23-54-25 43-52-44-44-23-35 42-22-25-23-43-53 52-43 22-52-31 22-51 31-53-23 53-22-1-23. 55-41-35 31-53-23-13 25-22-44-35 53-34-15 31-22 31-53-23 34-25-53-15-55-23-44-34-31-23-25 51-22-54 31-45-23-41-31-13 43-34-23-12-23-25 22-51 25-34-44-33-23-54, 55-41-35 31-53-23-13 31-22-22-11 42-22-25-23-43-53 31-22 23-21-13-43-31.

Genesis 37:28 NLV

THE BIBLE'S BOOK OF GENESIS: JOSEPH EXPLAINS THE KING OF EGYPT'S DREAM

Joseph said to Pharaoh, "Pharaoh's dreams are one and the same.
God has shown Pharaoh what He is about to do."

Genesis 41:25 NLV

Joseph loved and served God. But his life was hard. First, Joseph was a slave to an important official of Egypt. Then Joseph was accused of something he didn't do—and he was thrown into jail! But God helped Joseph explain the dreams of two other prisoners. Before long, he was called to explain the dream of Egypt's king, the pharaoh. A terrible famine was coming, and Egypt should store up food for that time. Pharaoh was so impressed that he made Joseph second-in-command of all Egypt! Then Joseph forgave his brothers and took care of them in Egypt.

17. JOSEPH EXPLAINS PHARAOH'S DREAM — WORD SEARCH

And **Pharaoh** said to **Joseph**, "I have dreamed a **dream**, and there is **none** who can **interpret** it, and I have **heard** it said of you that you can **understand** a dream to interpret it." And Joseph **answered** Pharaoh, **saying**, "It is not in me. **God** shall **give** Pharaoh an answer of **peace**."
GENESIS 41:15–16 SKJV

U	I	H	M	M	P	E	A	C	E
H	N	D	E	R	E	W	S	N	A
O	T	D	R	E	A	M	F	B	R
A	E	L	E	P	N	M	N	H	V
R	R	G	M	R	M	O	H	X	H
A	P	B	N	Y	S	P	N	E	N
H	R	D	L	I	E	T	A	E	E
P	E	O	Q	S	Y	R	A	V	F
Z	T	G	O	K	D	A	I	N	W
B	J	J	L	F	V	G	S	T	D

18. JOSEPH FORGIVES HIS BROTHERS — ACROSTIC

All Quotations SKJV

What Joseph and Egypt did when Jacob died (Genesis 50:3)	22-12-3-25-17-27-19
"And Joseph went up to ___ his father" (Genesis 50:7)	2-3-18-8
With their father dead, Joseph's brothers thought he would ___ them (Genesis 50:15)	29-14-4-24
What the brothers asked Joseph to do (Genesis 50:17)	30-7-11-21-10-6-20
Joseph said to them, "Do not fear, for am I in the ___ of God?" (Genesis 50:19)	5-1-26-28-13
God planned for Joseph to "___ many people alive" (Genesis 50:20)	16-31-6-9

"2-3-4 31-16 30-7-11 8-12-3, 8-12-3 4-29-7-3-21-29-4 9-23-10-1 14-21-26-10-17-16-4 22-27, 2-3-4 21-12-19 22-13-14-17-4 10-4 30-7-18 21-12-7-19, 4-7 2-25-10-17-21 4-7 5-26-16-16, 26-16 10-4 10-16 4-29-10-16 19-31-8, 4-12 16-14-6-24 22-26-17-8 5-9-12-5-1-20 14-1-10-23-13."
GENESIS 50:20 SKJV

THE BIBLE'S BOOK OF EXODUS: GOD SPEAKS TO MOSES FROM A BURNING BUSH

God called to him from inside the bush, saying, "Moses, Moses!" Moses answered, "Here I am." God said, "Do not come near. Take your shoes off your feet. For the place where you are standing is holy ground."

Exodus 3:4–5 NLV

Jacob's family did well in Egypt. But when Joseph died, a new pharaoh was afraid of the growing family. So the king made the people his slaves. God heard the Israelites' groaning. He remembered His promises to Abraham, Isaac, and Jacob. God chose Moses to rescue the people from slavery. God spoke to Moses through a burning bush. Though he was afraid, Moses agreed to tell Pharaoh to let God's people go.

19. MOSES AND THE BURNING BUSH — CROSSWORD

All Quotations SKJV

Across

2 What Moses was watching when the Lord called him (Exodus 3:1)

4 The Lord said, "I am the God of your ____" (Exodus 3:6)

5 The mountain of God was called ____ (Exodus 3:1)

6 Moses' father-in-law's name was ____ (Exodus 3:1)

Down

1 ____ called Moses from inside the bush (Exodus 3:4)

2 There was a ____ inside the bush, but it was not burning up (Exodus 3:2)

3 God told Moses to take his ____ off (Exodus 3:5)

4 Moses hid his ____ because he was afraid to look at God (Exodus 3:7)

5 God said the ground Moses was standing on was ____ (Exodus 3:5)

20. GOD PUNISHES EGYPT — DECODER

	1	2	3	4	5
1	D	L	O	F	M
2	G	W	J	S	P
3	R	I	B	T	A
4	C	U	N	V	Y
5	Q	K	E	X	H

34-55-53 12-13-31-11 24-35-32-11 34-13 15-13-24-53-24. . . "25-55-35-31-35-13-55 22-32-12-12 43-13-34 12-32-24-34-53-43 34-13 45-13-42. 34-55-53-43 32 22-32-12-12 12-35-45 15-45 55-35-43-11 13-43 53-21-45-25-34. 33-45 21-31-53-35-34 35-41-34-24 34-55-35-34 22-32-12-12 25-42-43-32-24-55 34-55-53 53-21-45-25-34-32-35-43-24, 32 22-32-12-12 33-31-32-43-21 13-42-34 15-45 14-35-15-32-12-45 21-31-13-42-25-24, 15-45 25-53-13-25-12-53, 34-55-53 24-13-43-24 13-14 32-24-31-35-53-12, 14-31-13-15 34-55-53 12-35-43-11 13-14 53-21-45-25-34. 34-55-53 53-21-45-25-34-32-35-43-24 22-32-12-12 52-43-13-22 34-55-35-34 32 35-15 34-55-53 12-13-31-11 22-55-53-43 32 25-42-34 15-45 55-35-43-11 42-25-13-43 53-21-45-25-34 35-43-11 33-31-32-43-21 13-42-34 34-55-53 25-53-13-25-12-53 13-14 32-24-31-35-53-12 14-31-13-15 35-15-13-43-21 34-55-53-15."

EXODUS 7:1, 4–5 NLV

THE BIBLE'S BOOK OF EXODUS: MOSES SPLITS THE RED SEA IN TWO!

Then the Lord said to Moses, "Why do you cry to me? Tell the people of Israel to keep going. Lift up your special stick and put out your hand over the sea, and divide it. Then the people of Israel will go through the sea on dry land."

EXODUS 14:15–16 NLV

God sent ten terrible plagues on Egypt to convince Pharaoh to let the Israelites go. The last plague was the death of every firstborn child—except those of God's people. They put the blood of a sacrificed lamb on their doorposts so the Lord would "pass over" their homes. Pharaoh finally let the Israelites leave, in an event called "the Exodus." God used Moses to split the Red Sea in two for His people to escape from Egypt.

21. THE TENTH—AND WORST—PLAGUE ON EGYPT — WORD SEARCH

Moses said, "The **Lord** says this: 'About **midnight** I will go through **Egypt**. And all the first-born in the land of Egypt will **die**, from the first-born of **Pharaoh** who sits on his **throne** to the first-born of the **servant** girl grinding the grain, and even the first-born of the **cattle**. There will be loud **crying** in all the land of Egypt, more than has ever been **heard** before or will ever be heard **again**.

EXODUS 11:4–6 NLV

```
T R E G M K T D N G
K N T G K G R S R E
Q F A G Y O D E A L
C D H V L P P S G T
R I J E R H T O A T
Y E T Z A E R M I A
I M G R N R S R N C
N K A K N N D B N K
G O M I D N I G H T
H F E N O R H T W F
```

22. PARTING THE RED SEA — ACROSTIC

All Quotations NLV

What Moses held in his hand to divide the sea (Exodus 14:16)	11-27-30-4-21
The people who were chasing the people of Israel (Exodus 14:17)	22-38-2-35-16-41-9-31-25
What moved from in front of the people to behind them? (Exodus 14:19)	7-45-19-32-14
What came off the war-wagons? (Exodus 14:25)	39-10-24-17-46-5
The time of day that the horses and horsemen went into the sea (Exodus 14:24)	20-36-6-29-40-15-44
The Egyptian army was _____ (Exodus 14:24)	42-12-33-26-1-23
The Israelites "_____ in the Lord" (Exodus 14:31)	37-3-34-28-13-43-18-8

37-32-27 27-10-24 35-17-19-35-45-3 36-12 30-11-33-42-13-46 39-26-34-21-18-23 19-29 14-6-2 45-42-15-23

27-10-33-36-32-44-10 27-10-24 5-17-26. 27-10-3 39-26-27-13-6-11 39-18-33-24 46-40-21-17 42 39-26-34-45 27-19

27-10-3-20 36-29 27-10-13-1-6 33-28-44-10-27 42-15-8 19-15 27-10-18-30-6 45-24-12-27.

EXODUS 14:29 NLV

THE BIBLE'S BOOK OF EXODUS: GOD GIVES THE TEN COMMANDMENTS TO MOSES

Then God spoke all these words, saying, "I am the Lord your God, Who brought you out of the land of Egypt, out of the house where you were servants. "Have no gods other than Me."

Exodus 20:1–3 NLV

At Mount Sinai, God gave Moses the Ten Commandments. There were also rules for worshipping God, and laws to change the family into a nation. When Moses stayed many days on the mountain, the people did something really foolish: they worshipped a golden calf. Moses came back to set things right. The book of Exodus ends with the people traveling to their "promised land" of Canaan. They followed God's "pillar of the cloud" by day and "pillar of fire" by night.

23. THE TEN COMMANDMENTS — CROSSWORD

All Quotations SKJV

Across

2 "You shall not desire your neighbor's ____" (Deuteronomy 5:21)

6 "Keep the ____ day to sanctify it" (Deuteronomy 5:12)

8 "You shall not bear ____ witness against your neighbor" (Deuteronomy 5:20)

9 "You shall not take the ____ of the LORD your God in vain" (Deuteronomy 5:11)

Down

1 "You shall not ____" (Deuteronomy 5:17)

3 "You shall not make for yourself any ____ image" (Deuteronomy 5:8)

4 "You shall have no other ____ before Me" (Deuteronomy 5:7)

5 "You shall not ____ adultery" (Deuteronomy 5:18)

7 "____ your father and your mother" (Deuteronomy 5:16)

24. DO WHAT GOD SAYS! — DECODER

	1	2	3	4	5
1	I	E	R	N	C
2	P	L	V	A	H
3	B	X	G	T	W
4	O	J	Z	Y	K
5	F	U	S	D	M

"34-25-12-13-12-51-41-13-12 44-41-52 53-25-24-22-22 31-12 15-24-13-12-51-52-22 34-41 54-41 24-53 34-25-12 22-41-13-54 44-41-52-13 33-41-54 25-24-53 15-41-55-55-24-14-54-12-54 44-41-52. 44-41-52 53-25-24-22-22 14-41-34 34-52-13-14 24-53-11-54-12 34-41 34-25-12 13-11-33-25-34 25-24-14-54 41-13 34-41 34-25-12 22-12-51-34."

DEUTERONOMY 5:32 SKJV

THE BIBLE'S BOOK OF JOSHUA: THE WALLS OF JERICHO FALL DOWN!

So the people called out and the religious leaders blew the horns. When the people heard the sound of the horns, they called out even louder. And the wall fell to the ground. All the people went straight in and took the city.

Joshua 6:20 NLV

It took God's people a long time to reach their promised land. Because they complained and sinned, God made them wander in the wilderness for forty years! Moses had died, so Joshua led the people into Canaan. The city of Jericho stood in the Israelites' way. But God knocked its thick walls flat as Joshua's army marched outside, blowing trumpets and shouting. Joshua fought many battles to clear the idol-worshipping people out of the land.

25. BATTLE OF JERICHO — ACROSTIC

All Quotations NLV

The number of religious leaders and rams' horns (Joshua 6:4)	8-23-17-35-3
Israel's leader, the son of Nun (Joshua 6:6)	38-5-33-20-13-29
"Take up the _____ box of the agreement" (Joshua 6:6)	28-15-2-39-24-10-27
The leaders _____ the rams' horns (Joshua 6:8)	34-7-40-25
"Joshua got up early in the _____" (Joshua 6:12)	14-21-11-30-4-36-18
The city was to be _____ (Joshua 6:17)	19-37-16-41-6-22-31-12-42
On the seventh day, the wall _____ (Joshua 16:20)	1-26-9-32

41-20-23 8-35-17-2-3-41-20 41-24-14-40, 25-20-37-30 41-20-12 11-26-27-4-18-24-21-13-33 9-23-29-42-35-6-28 34-32-2-25 41-20-40-4-11 20-22-6-36-16, 38-21-8-20-13-10 33-10-24-19 41-22 41-20-37 15-12-21-15-27-26, "39-29-7-9 22-13-41! 1-21-6 41-20-23 32-22-11-19 20-10-28 18-4-17-35-3 31-21-13 41-20-2 39-24-41-31."
JOSHUA 6:16 NLV

26. JOSHUA'S LAST ADVICE FOR ISRAEL — WORD SEARCH

"**Fear** the Lord. **Serve** Him in **faith** and **truth**. Put away the **gods** your fathers served on the other side of the **river** and in **Egypt**. Serve the Lord. If you think it is wrong to serve the Lord, **choose** today whom you will serve. Choose the gods your fathers **worshiped** on the other side of the river, or choose the gods of the **Amorites** in whose **land** you are **living**. But as for me and my **family**, we will serve the **Lord**."
JOSHUA 24:14–15 NLV

```
F A I T H T R T K D
R G L R L Y R N D E
A K D I L Y E U S P
E Y N I V V T E T I
F S M K R I T P R H
L A O E V I N I G S
F O S O R F V G O R
V P R O H E T T D O
C V M D R C W G S W
L A N D J T P Y G E
```

THE BIBLE'S BOOK OF JUDGES: SAMSON DESTROYS THE ENEMY'S TEMPLE

Then Samson called to the Lord and said, "O Lord God, I beg You. Remember me. Give me strength only this once, O God. So I may now punish the Philistines for my two eyes." Samson took hold of the two center pillars that held up the building. He pushed against them, with his right hand on one and his left hand on the other. Samson said, "Let me die with the Philistines!" Then he pushed with all his strength so that the building fell on the leaders and all the people in it.

JUDGES 16:28–30 NLV

After Joshua died, the Israelites began to worship idols. So God sent enemies to punish them. When they cried out, God sent rescuers called "judges." Some famous judges are Deborah, the only woman judge, and the amazingly strong Samson. But Samson made many bad choices. He died knocking down a Philistine temple.

27. JUDGE DEBORAH GOES INTO BATTLE — DECODER

24-23-21 11-22-43-43-35-31-23-32-42 ' 12 21-35-55-15 31-15-44-23-54-22-42, 22 21-23-45-22-24 21-42-23 12-43-23-33-15 55-23-54 13-23-31, 21-22-12 51-25-31-13-35-24-13 35-12-54-22-15-11 22-32 32-42-22-32 32-35-45-15. . . . 12-42-15 12-15-24-32 55-23-54 44-22-54-22-33 . . . 22-24-31 12-22-35-31 32-23 42-35-45, "32-42-15 11-23-54-31, 32-42-15 13-23-31 23-55 35-12-54-22-15-11, 12-22-41-12, '13-23 32-23 45-23-25-24-32 32-22-44-23-54.'" . . . 44-22-54-22-33 12-22-35-31 32-23 42-15-54, "35 21-35-11-11 13-23 35-55 41-23-25 13-23 21-35-32-42 45-15. 44-25-32 35-55 41-23-25 31-23 24-23-32 13-23 21-35-32-42 45-15, 35 21-35-11-11 24-23-32 13-23." 22-24-31 12-42-15 12-22-35-31, "55-23-54 12-25-54-15 35 21-35-11-11 13-23 21-35-32-42 41-23-25. 44-25-32 32-42-15 42-23-24-23-54 21-35-11-11 24-23-32 44-15 41-23-25-54-12 22-12 41-23-25 13-23 23-24 41-23-25-54 21-22-41."

JUDGES 4:4, 6, 8–9 NLV

	1	2	3	4	5
1	L	S	G	Q	E
2	W	A	O	N	U
3	D	T	K	X	I
4	Y	H	P	B	M
5	J	C	V	R	F

28. SAMSON'S DEATH — CROSSWORD

All Quotations SKJV

■	■	■	■	■	1	■	2	■	■
■	3	■	4					■	■
■		■		■		■		■	5
■		■		■		■		■	
■		■		■	■	6			
■	7					■	■	■	
■		■	■	■	■	■	■	■	
■		■	■	■	■	■	■	■	
8						■	■	■	
■	■	■	■	■	■	■	■	■	■

Across

4 "He killed more at his ____ than he killed in his life" (Judges 16:30)

6 "Then he pushed with all his strength so that the building ____" (Judges 16:30)

7 What Philistine leaders gave Delilah to learn Samon's secret (Judges 16:18)

8 Samson was put in a Philistine ____ (Judges 16:21)

Down

1 Samson's had never been cut (Judges 16:17)

2 Number of times Samson lied to Delilah about the source of his strength (Judges 16:15)

3 What Samson asked God to do for him (Judges 16:28)

4 False god of the Philistines (Judges 16:23)

5 "Samson took hold of the two center ____ that held up the building" (Judges 16:29)

THE BIBLE'S BOOK OF RUTH: RUTH PICKS UP GRAIN IN THE FIELD OF BOAZ

So Ruth went and gathered in the field behind those who picked the grain. And she happened to come to the part of the field that belonged to Boaz, who was of the family of Elimelech.

RUTH 2:3 NLV

Ruth was a Gentile—that means she was not part of God's chosen people, the Israelites. But she married into an Israelite family. When all of the men of the family died, Ruth stuck with her mother-in-law, Naomi. Ruth picked up leftover grain in a rich man's field to keep herself and Naomi alive. Before long, Boaz married Ruth—who would start a family line that included King David and Jesus Christ!

29. RUTH AND BOAZ MEET — ACROSTIC

All Quotations NLV

Boaz came from _____ (Ruth 2:4)	10-35-24-1-33-21-7-16-27
Boaz said, "May the Lord be with _____" (Ruth 2:4)	4-15-23
"Ruth went and _____ in the field" (Ruth 2:3)	28-9-30-18-5-32-37-11
"May the Lord reward you for your _____" (Ruth 2:12)	20-12-36-2
"I have found _____ in your eyes" (Ruth 2:13)	31-8-25-19-14
Boaz was kind in the way he was _____ to Ruth (Ruth 2:13)	17-26-3-29-13-22-34-6

17-15 32-23-30-1 28-9-24-18-35-36-21-11 6-14-8-22-34 22-34 30-1-16 31-22-5-33-11 23-34-24-22-33

37-25-3-34-22-34-28. 30-18-37-34 17-1-5 10-16-29-24 12-23-30 20-18-9-24 17-1-21 18-8-11 6-29-30-1-35-32-21-11.

22-24 20-9-17 16-34-19-23-28-18 10-8-36-33-5-4 30-15 31-22-33-33 29 10-9-17-2-37-24.

Ruth 2:17 NLV

30. RUTH AND BOAZ START A FAMILY — WORD SEARCH

N	W	I	F	E	C	Y	K	R	C
C	S	R	O	B	H	G	I	E	N
R	T	G	B	G	J	W	P	H	D
L	F	R	O	L	O	C	D	T	A
N	O	J	R	M	M	E	Q	A	V
N	T	R	E	T	B	Z	M	F	I
A	N	N	D	O	H	A	N	A	D
O	O	F	M	T	N	O	T	P	N
M	S	W	U	T	R	B	Q	K	P
I	F	R	Y	K	J	E	S	S	E

So **Boaz** took **Ruth**, and she was his **wife**. And when he went in to her, the **Lord** gave her conception, and she **bore** a son. . . . And the **women**, her **neighbors**, gave it a **name**, saying, "There is a **son** born to **Naomi**," and they called his name **Obed**. He is the **father** of **Jesse**, the father of **David**.

Ruth 4:13, 17 SKJV

THE BIBLE'S BOOK OF 1 SAMUEL: THE PROPHET SAMUEL ANOINTS SAUL TO BE KING

Then Samuel took a bottle of oil and poured it on Saul's head. He kissed him and said, "Has not the Lord chosen you to be a ruler over His land?"

1 Samuel 10:1 NLV

A miracle baby named Samuel grew up to be a judge and prophet of Israel. Samuel was very good, but his sons were very bad. So the people of Israel asked him for a king. God told Samuel to find the tall and handsome Saul to be Israel's first ruler. King Saul started well but began making poor choices. Before long, God had a message for Saul. Samuel told the king that he would be replaced.

31. SAMUEL AND SAUL — CROSSWORD

All Quotations NLV

Across

2 Saul was a "good-looking ____ man" (1 Samuel 9:2)

4 God said to Samuel, "Choose him to be the ____ of My people Israel" (1 Samuel 9:16)

6 Samuel took a bottle of ___ and poured it on Saul's head (1 Samuel 10:1)

8 Saul found Samuel, "the ___ of God" (1 Samuel 9:11)

9 Saul was searching for his father's lost _____ when he met Samuel (1 Samuel 9:3)

Down

1 God told Samuel that Saul "is the one who will ____ over My people" (1 Samuel 9:17)

3 The land where Saul was from (1 Samuel 9:16)

5 Saul and Samuel spoke on the ____ (1 Samuel 9:25)

7 Samuel told Saul, "I will make the ____ of God known to you" (1 Samuel 9:27)

32. SAMUEL AND SAUL — DECODER

	1	2	3	4	5
1	E	H	W	T	G
2	N	S	B	K	Z
3	L	J	X	O	C
4	Y	D	R	V	I
5	F	P	U	M	A

55-21-42 13-12-11-21 22-55-54-53-11-31 22-55-13 22-55-53-31, 14-12-11 31-34-43-42 22-55-45-42 14-34 12-45-54, "23-11-12-34-31-42 14-12-11 54-55-21 13-12-34-54 45 22-52-34-24-11 34-51 14-34 41-34-53! 14-12-45-22 22-55-54-11 54-55-21 22-12-55-31-31 43-11-45-15-21 34-44-11-43 54-41 52-11-34-52-31-11."

1 Samuel 9:17 SKJV

THE BIBLE'S BOOK OF 1 SAMUEL: YOUNG DAVID FIGHTS A GIANT

Then David said to the Philistine, "You come to me with a sword and spears. But I come to you in the name of the Lord of All, the God of the armies of Israel, Whom you have stood against. This day the Lord will give you into my hands."

1 Samuel 17:45–46 NLV

The next king after Saul would be a young shepherd named David. With God's help, David used a sling and a stone to defeat a giant Philistine warrior named Goliath. David became Israel's hero, but the jealous King Saul wanted to kill him.

33. DAVID AND HIS SLING — ACROSTIC

All Quotations SKJV

Goliath was a _____ (1 Samuel 17:4) 25-34-3-28-11-38-8-14

Goliath's height "was six _____ and a span" (1 Samuel 17:4) 19-35-9-32-17-37

Goliath was from _____ (1 Samuel 17:23) 1-22-13-30

Saul and the Israelite men camped in the _____ of Elah (1 Samuel 17:2) 29-15-6-20-33-27

David gathered this many stones for his sling (1 Samuel 17:40) 12-36-4-23

David found the stones in the _____ (1 Samuel 17:40) 31-10-24-2-18

David did not have a _____ (1 Samuel 17:50) 21-7-16-26-5

15-14-5 7-30-23-14 13-34-33 11-30-36-6-32-21-17-38-14-23 20-8-24-18-33-5 22-10-2-35-14-5 3-14-5 37-22-7

5-15-4-32-5, 34-23 5-38-21-5-3-36-14-33-5 30-32-28, 12-16-10 34-23 7-15-37 8-14-6-27 22 27-24-35-13-30,

3-14-5 10-35-5-5-27 22-14-5 34-15-5 3 30-15-14-5-21-2-28-33 12-22-19-23.

1 Samuel 17:42 SKJV

34. JEALOUS KING SAUL — WORD SEARCH

```
G S R D E Y A L P E
N D D Y R G N A N G
I A R N G Q G I T R
L N O S A N T V R D
L C N W I S L K U I
I I O K I N U H S V
K N H L S K G O T A
H G I A M R C I H D
Z H U W O M E N N T
P L J E A L O U S G
```

When David returned from **killing** the **Philistine**, the **women** came out of all the cities of Israel, **singing** and **dancing**, to meet King **Saul**, playing songs of joy on timbrels. The women sang as they **played**, and said, "Saul has killed his **thousands**, and **David** his ten thousands." Then Saul became very **angry**. This saying did not please him. He said, "They have given David **honor** for ten thousands, but for me only thousands. Now what more can he have but to be **king**?" And Saul was **jealous** and did not **trust** David from that day on.

1 Samuel 18:6–9 NLV

THE BIBLE'S BOOK OF 1 SAMUEL: DAVID AND JONATHAN, BEST FRIENDS

Jonathan said to David, "Go in peace. For we have promised each other in the name of the Lord, saying, 'The Lord will be between me and you, and between my children and your children forever.'" Then David got up and left, and Jonathan went into the city.

1 Samuel 20:42 NLV

Saul's son Jonathan loved David. They were best friends, and Jonathan tried to protect David. When David had a chance to kill Saul, he would not. Saul died in battle against the Philistines. Jonathan also died in that battle.

35. DAVID AND JONATHAN — CROSSWORD

All Quotations NLV

Across

3 David told Jonathan, "There is only a step between me and ____" (1 Samuel 20:3)

5 Saul threw his ____ at Jonathan to kill him (1 Samuel 20:33)

8 David made a ____ to Jonathan (1 Samuel 20:17)

9 David ____ in a field (1 Samuel 20:24)

Down

1 Saul said to Jonathan that the son of ____ "must die" (1 Samuel 20:30–31)

2 Jonathan loved David "as he loved his own ____" (1 Samuel 20:17)

4 Number of arrows Jonathan planned to shoot as a message to David (1 Samuel 20:20)

6 How Saul felt about his son Jonathan's friendship with David (1 Samuel 20:30)

7 David and Jonathan ____ when they parted (1 Samuel 20:41)

36. DAVID BECOMES KING — DECODER

	1	2	3	4	5
1	F	M	V	K	D
2	J	A	Y	T	O
3	R	P	L	E	W
4	C	U	G	X	Q
5	I	N	S	B	H

22-52-15 24-55-34 12-34-52 25-11 21-42-15-22-55 41-22-12-34, 22-52-15 24-55-34-31-34 24-55-34-23 22-52-25-51-52-24-34-15 15-22-13-51-15 14-51-52-43 25-13-34-31 24-55-34 55-25-42-53-34 25-11 21-42-15-22-55. 22-52-15 24-55-34-23 24-25-33-15 15-22-13-51-15, 53-22-23-51-52-43, "24-55-34 12-34-52 25-11 21-22-54-34-53-55 – 43-51-33-34-22-15 35-34-31-34 24-55-25-53-34 35-55-25 54-42-31-51-34-15 53-22-42-33." 22-52-15 15-22-13-51-15 53-34-52-24 12-34-53-53-34-52-43-34-31-53 . . . 22-52-15 53-22-51-15 24-25 24-55-34-12, "23-25-42 22-31-34 54-33-34-53-53-34-15 25-11 24-55-34 33-25-31-15 24-55-22-24 23-25-42 55-22-13-34 53-55-25-35-52 24-55-51-53 14-51-52-15-52-34-53-53 24-25 23-25-42-31 33-25-31-15, 34-13-34-52 24-25 53-22-42-33, 22-52-15 55-22-13-34 54-42-31-51-34-15 55-51-12. 22-52-15 52-25-35 12-22-23 24-55-34 33-25-31-15 53-55-25-35 14-51-52-15-52-34-53-53 22-52-15 24-31-42-24-55 24-25 23-25-42."

2 Samuel 2:4–7 skjv

THE BIBLE'S BOOK OF 1 KINGS: KING SOLOMON SHOWS HIS WISDOM

And the king said, "Divide the living child in two. Give half to the one woman and half to the other." Then the mother of the living child had much pity for her son and said to the king, "O, my lord, give her the living child. Do not kill him." But the other woman said, "He will not be mine or yours. Divide him." Then the king answered and said, "Give the first woman the living child. Do not kill him. She is his mother."

1 Kings 3:25–27 NLV

David was a very good king in Israel. He ruled for forty years. When David died, his son Solomon became king. God spoke to Solomon in a dream, offering him anything he'd like—and Solomon chose wisdom. God gave Solomon great wisdom, along with much power and wealth. Solomon built God a beautiful house of worship in Jerusalem. But he also began to marry many different women, and they turned his heart away from God. When Solomon died, his kingdom divided into two parts. The north was still called Israel; the south was called Judah.

37. SOLOMON CHOOSES WISDOM — DECODER

	1	2	3	4	5
1	W	F	R	I	L
2	N	Z	Y	B	P
3	A	X	E	T	G
4	V	M	S	O	D
5	K	U	C	H	J

"24-33-53-31-52-43-33 23-44-52 54-31-41-33 31-43-51-33-45 34-54-14-43, 14 54-31-41-33 45-44-21-33 11-54-31-34 23-44-52 43-31-14-45. 43-33-33, 14 54-31-41-33 35-14-41-33-21 23-44-52 31 11-14-43-33 31-21-45 52-21-45-33-13-43-34-31-21-45-14-21-35 54-33-31-13-34. 21-44 44-21-33 54-31-43 24-33-33-21 15-14-51-33 23-44-52 24-33-12-44-13-33, 31-21-45 34-54-33-13-33 11-14-15-15 24-33 21-44 44-21-33 15-14-51-33 23-44-52 14-21 34-54-33 12-52-34-52-13-33. 14 35-14-41-33 23-44-52 11-54-31-34 23-44-52 54-31-41-33 21-44-34 31-43-51-33-45, 31-15-43-44. 14 35-14-41-33 23-44-52 24-44-34-54 13-14-53-54-33-43 31-21-45 54-44-21-44-13. 43-44 34-54-33-13-33 11-14-15-15 24-33 21-44 51-14-21-35 15-14-51-33 23-44-52 31-15-15 23-44-52-13 45-31-23-43. 31-21-45 14-12 23-44-52 11-31-15-51 14-21 42-23 11-31-23-43 31-21-45 51-33-33-25 42-23 15-31-11-43 31-21-45 11-44-13-45 31-43 23-44-52-13 12-31-34-54-33-13 45-31-41-14-45 45-14-45, 14 11-14-15-15 31-15-15-44-11 23-44-52 34-44 15-14-41-33 31 15-44-21-35 34-14-42-33."

1 Kings 3:11–14 NLV

38. ISRAEL SPLITS IN TWO — WORD SEARCH

```
K J E R U S A L E M
D F A M I L Y E M R
S A E S U O H A K E
R T V V H Z R R M H
Q H N I M O N S Q O
S A T E D E J I J B
H D J A T E V Z R O
A U M S S K I N G A
R J I S B W O R K M
E L E D E L L I K M
```

All **Israel** saw that the king did not **listen** to them. So they said to the **king**, "What share do we have in **David**? We have no **share** in the son of **Jesse**! To your tents, O Israel! Now look after your own **house**, David!" So Israel went to their **tents**. But as for the people of Israel who lived in the cities of **Judah**, Rehoboam ruled over them. Then King **Rehoboam** sent **Adoram**, who ruled over those who were made to **work**, and all Israel **killed** him with stones. So King Rehoboam got on his war-wagon in a hurry to go to **Jerusalem**. So Israel turned against the **family** of David to this day.

1 Kings 12:16–19 NLV

THE BIBLE'S BOOKS OF KINGS: THE PROPHET ELIJAH BEATS THE PROPHETS OF BAAL

Elijah the man who spoke for God came near and said, "O Lord, God of Abraham, Isaac and Israel, let it be known today that You are God in Israel. Let it be known that I am Your servant, and have done all these things at Your word. Answer me, O Lord. Answer me so these people may know that You, O Lord, are God. Turn their hearts to You again." Then the fire of the Lord fell.

1 Kings 18:36–38 NLV

God had a prophet named Elijah. He would tell God's words to people—even to the evil King Ahab and Queen Jezebel of Israel. They worshipped a false god called Baal. In the real God's power, Elijah defeated 450 prophets of Baal in a fiery contest on Mount Carmel.

39. ELIJAH AND THE FALSE PROPHETS — CROSSWORD

All Quotations KJV

Across

2 The false prophets called on their god, but "there was no ____" (1 Kings 18:26)

6 "____ me, O Lord," Elijah prayed (1 Kings 18:37)

7 Elijah told King Ahab to send the prophets of ____ (1 Kings 18:19)

8 What Elijah built for the sacrifices (1 Kings 18:32)

Down

1 What the true God sent down to prove Himself (1 Kings 18:38)

3 Israel was to gather at Mount ____ (1 Kings 18:19)

4 Animal to be offered as a sacrifice (1 Kings 18:25)

5 What Elijah poured over the sacrifice (1 Kings 18:33–35)

40. ELIJAH GOES TO HEAVEN WITHOUT DYING! — DECODER

	1	2	3	4	5
1	C	G	M	T	A
2	P	J	O	X	F
3	Z	B	V	I	R
4	E	S	Y	L	U
5	K	N	D	W	H

15-52-53 34-14 11-15-13-41 14-23 21-15-42-42, 15-42 14-55-41-43 42-14-34-44-44 54-41-52-14 23-52, 15-52-53 14-15-44-51-41-53, 14-55-15-14, 32-41-55-23-44-53, 14-55-41-35-41 15-21-21-41-15-35-41-53 15 11-55-15-35-34-23-14 23-25 25-34-35-41, 15-52-53 55-23-35-42-41-42 23-25 25-34-35-41, 15-52-53 21-15-35-14-41-53 14-55-41-13 32-23-14-55 15-42-45-52-53-41-35; 15-52-53 41-44-34-22-15-55 54-41-52-14 45-21 32-43 15 54-55-34-35-44-54-34-52-53 34-52-14-23 55-41-15-33-41-52. 15-52-53 41-44-34-42-55-15 42-15-54 34-14, 15-52-53 55-41 11-35-34-41-53, 13-43 25-15-14-55-41-35, 13-43 25-15-14-55-41-35, 14-55-41 11-55-15-35-34-23-14 23-25 34-42-35-15-41-44, 15-52-53 14-55-41 55-23-35-42-41-13-41-52 14-55-41-35-41-23-25.

2 Kings 2:11–12 KJV

THE BIBLE'S BOOKS OF KINGS: AN EIGHT-YEAR-OLD KING!

Josiah was eight years old when he became king. He ruled for thirty-one years in Jerusalem. His mother's name was Jedidah the daughter of Adaiah of Bozkath. Josiah did what is right in the eyes of the Lord. He walked in all the way of his father David. He did not turn aside to the right or to the left.

2 Kings 22:1–2 NLV

God's people did many things wrong. Prophets like Elijah and Elisha tried to warn them, but they didn't always listen. In Israel, every king was wicked. God sent an enemy called Assyria to destroy Israel. Judah had a few good kings, like Hezekiah and Josiah. As a nation, Judah lasted a few years longer. But then it was attacked and ruined by the country called Babylon. Its soldiers broke up the walls around Jerusalem and burned much of the city.

41. JOSIAH, THE BOY KING — WORD SEARCH

Josiah was **eight** years old when he began to **reign**, and he reigned thirty-one years in **Jerusalem**. And his mother's name was **Jedidah** the daughter of Adaiah of Bozkath. And he did what was **right** in the **sight** of the **Lord**, and **walked** in all the **ways** of his father **David**, and did not turn aside to the right hand or to the **left**.

2 Kings 22:1–2 SKJV

K	T	J	N	D	R	O	L	N	F
D	M	L	E	F	T	J	X	S	W
E	E	T	R	D	K	L	I	L	H
K	L	Q	I	T	I	G	R	T	A
L	A	G	G	Z	H	D	H	L	I
A	S	P	H	T	I	G	A	Y	S
W	U	X	T	V	I	S	F	H	O
K	R	R	A	E	N	J	Y	L	J
N	E	D	C	D	P	J	X	A	C
D	J	R	E	I	G	N	T	P	W

42. GOD FINALLY PUNISHES HIS PEOPLE FOR THEIR SIN — DECODER

	1	2	3	4	5
1	W	Q	M	U	J
2	O	A	T	F	H
3	K	B	L	Y	S
4	R	I	P	V	N
5	C	D	G	E	X

23-25-54-45 23-25-54 31-42-45-53 21-24 22-35-35-34-41-42-22 51-22-41-41-42-54-52 23-25-54 43-54-21-43-33-54 21-24 42-35-41-22-54-33 22-11-22-34 22-53-22-42-45-35-23 23-25-54-42-41 11-42-33-33 23-21 22-35-35-34-41-42-22. . . . 32-54-51-22-14-35-54 23-25-54 43-54-21-43-33-54 21-24 42-35-41-22-54-33 52-42-52 45-21-23 21-32-54-34 23-25-54 44-21-42-51-54 21-24 23-25-54 33-21-41-52 23-25-54-42-41 53-21-52. 23-25-54-34 35-42-45-45-54-52 22-53-22-42-45-35-23 25-42-35 22-53-41-54-54-13-54-45-23 22-45-52 54-44-54-45 22-33-33 23-25-22-23 23-25-54 33-21-41-52'35 35-54-41-44-22-45-23 13-21-35-54-35 23-21-33-52 23-25-54-13. 23-25-54-34 11-21-14-33-52 45-21-23 33-42-35-23-54-45 21-41 21-32-54-34.

2 Kings 18:11–12 NLV

THE BIBLE'S BOOK OF NEHEMIAH: FIXING THE BROKEN WALLS OF JERUSALEM

Those who were building the wall and those who carried loads did their work with one hand, and held something to fight with in the other hand. Each builder wore his sword at his side as he built. The man who blew the horn stood beside me.

Nehemiah 4:17–18 NLV

Nehemiah was one of God's people. But many of them now lived in Persia, not Israel. Nehemiah worked for the king of Persia. As a Jew, he was sad to learn that Jerusalem's walls were still broken down, many years after Babylon wrecked the city. Nehemiah got the king's permission to go to Jerusalem, where he led teams of workers in rebuilding the walls.

43. NEHEMIAH IN JERUSALEM — CROSSWORD

All Quotations KJV

Across

1 The walls were "____ down" (Nehemiah 2:13)

3 What had consumed Jerusalem's gates (Nehemiah 2:13)

5 Along with the horsemen, Persians who traveled to Jerusalem with Nehemiah (Nehemiah 2:13)

7 "The God of heaven, he will ____ us" (Nehemiah 2:20)

Down

2 What Nehemiah said the ruined city was (Nehemiah 2:17)

4 What Nehemiah called his people to do (Nehemiah 2:17)

6 Number of days Nehemiah scouted out Jerusalem (Nehemiah 2:11)

44. EXAMPLES OF THE WORK — WORD SEARCH

X	B	F	S	R	O	O	D	H	R
D	M	N	I	E	Y	L	S	H	S
T	B	R	G	D	N	I	H	R	D
J	O	U	H	A	F	M	E	D	J
N	J	O	I	E	T	H	E	E	E
J	L	R	M	L	T	E	P	R	R
Y	D	M	E	O	T	W	P	D	I
K	C	J	R	W	J	B	N	N	C
C	Y	B	C	W	O	R	K	U	H
W	O	O	D	Q	H	T	N	H	O

Then Eliashib the head religious **leader** and his **brothers** the religious leaders started to **work** and **built** the **Sheep** Gate. They set it apart as **holy**, and hung its **doors**. They set apart as holy the wall to the **Tower** of the **Hundred**, and to the Tower of Hananel. The men of **Jericho** built next to him. And Zaccur the son of Imri built next to them. The sons of Hassenaah built the **Fish** Gate. They laid the long **wood** pieces that hold up the **gate** and hung its doors with its **iron** pieces.
NEHEMIAH 3:1–3 NLV

THE BIBLE'S BOOK OF NEHEMIAH: A QUICK 52 DAYS OF REPAIRS

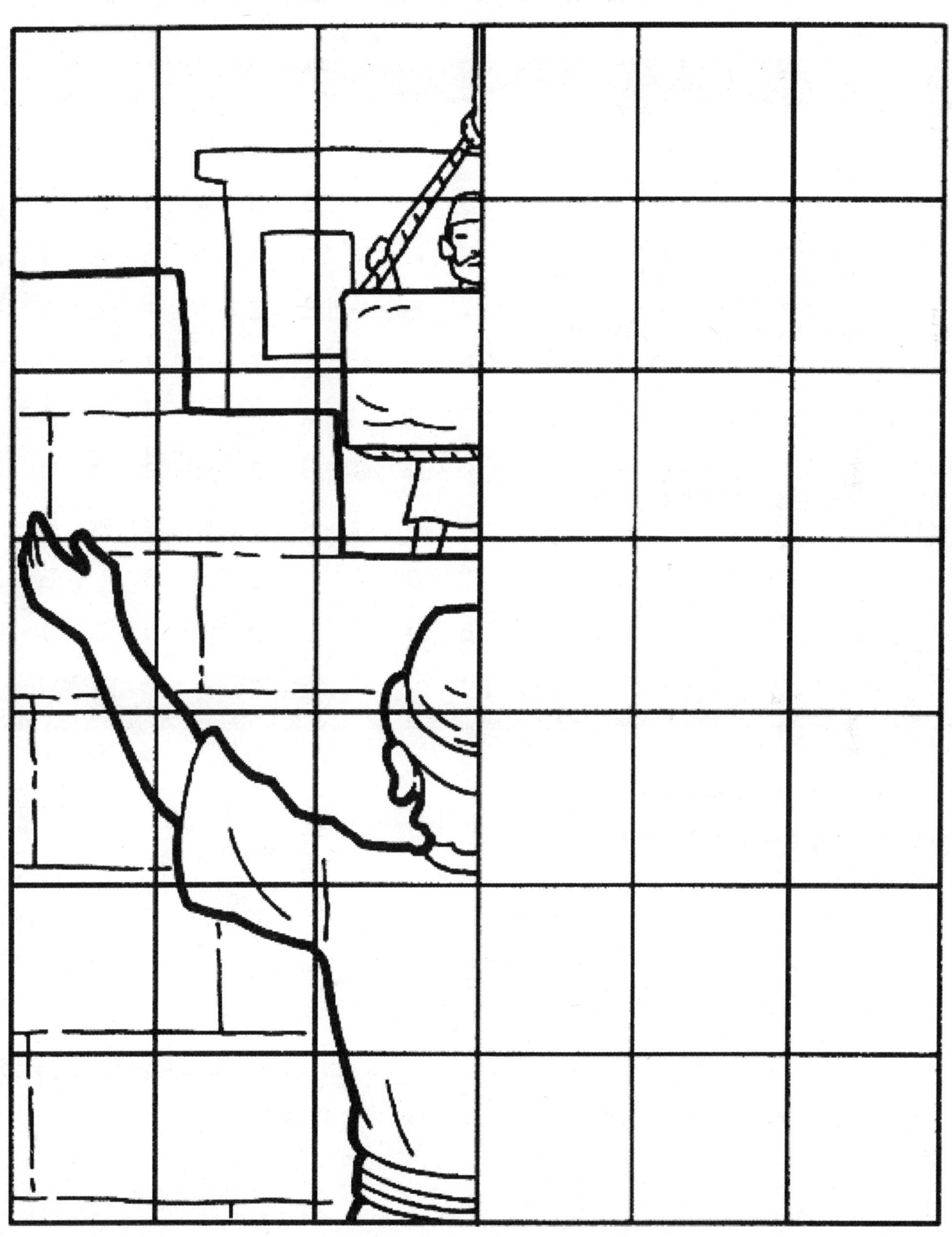

So we built the wall. . . . For the people had a mind to work.

NEHEMIAH 4:6 SKJV

Enemies of the Jews wanted to stop Nehemiah and his project. The workers would carry building tools in one hand and weapons in the other to keep themselves safe. And they finished their job in only fifty-two days! The quick work shocked the Jews' enemies, who realized that God had made it happen.

45. WORKERS AND FIGHTERS — WORD SEARCH

When those who **hated** us heard that it was known to us, and that **God** had brought **trouble** to their plan, then all of us **returned** to the **wall**. Each one returned to his **work**. From that day on, half of my **servants** did the work while half of them held the **spears**, battle-coverings, **bows**, and battle-clothes. And the **captains** stood behind the whole house of **Judah**. Those who were **building** the wall and those who **carried** loads did their work with one **hand**, and held something to **fight** with in the other hand.
NEHEMIAH 4:15–17 NLV

N	S	T	N	A	V	R	E	S	S
S	R	L	S	H	A	N	D	P	Z
N	D	R	D	W	Q	Q	E	J	B
I	E	L	E	Z	O	A	K	H	F
A	I	F	T	T	R	B	A	W	W
T	R	I	A	S	U	D	O	D	A
P	R	G	H	Z	U	R	O	N	L
A	A	H	R	J	K	G	N	G	L
C	C	T	R	O	U	B	L	E	L
B	U	I	L	D	I	N	G	J	D

46. SUCCESS! — ACROSTIC

All Quotations SKJV

"And they fortified _____" (Nehemiah 3:8) 31-7-24-17-35-4-37-13-29

The gate in Nehemiah 3:15 is the _____ Gate 5-28-11-22-36-8-32-18

The gate in Nehemiah 3:26 is the _____ Gate 33-2-25-15-29

One man who wanted to stop Nehemiah's work (Nehemiah 6:17) 12-26-9-19-3-34

The enemy's letters made Nehemiah feel _____ (Nehemiah 6:19) 23-14-6-21-10-30

"The _____ of Jerusalem was heard even from far away" (Nehemiah 12:43) 27-16-1

35-16 12-34-15 33-21-37-37 33-23-35 5-10-18-19-35-34-13-30 26-18 36-34-7 25-33-15-18-36-1 – 14-32-5-12-34 30-3-1 28-14 25-34-13 29-16-18-36-34 26-5 7-37-11-37, 10-18 14-19-5-12-1 – 25-33-28 30-2-1-35.

NEHEMIAH 6:15 SKJV

THE BIBLE'S BOOK OF ESTHER: BEAUTY QUEEN, QUEEN OF PERSIA

Esther was taken to King Ahasuerus in his royal house in the tenth month, which is the month of Tebeth, in the seventh year of his reign. And the king loved Esther more than all the women, and she obtained grace and favor in his sight more than all the virgins, so that he set the royal crown on her head and made her queen.

ESTHER 2:16–18 SKJV

A young Jewish woman becomes queen of Persia after winning a national beauty contest. But Esther didn't tell the king she was one of God's people. When an evil royal official wanted to kill every Jew in the country, Esther risked her own life to ask for the king's protection. The king was pleased with Esther and allowed the Jews to fight against their enemies. Esther's people won the battle and set up a holiday called Purim as a remembrance.

47. QUEEN ESTHER — CROSSWORD

All Quotations KJV

Across

2 Many maidens, including Esther, were brought to the ____ (Esther 2:8)

6 ____ could no longer be queen (Esther 1:19)

7 Esther's cousin, ____, raised her as his daughter (Esther 2:7)

Down

1 Esther was also called ____ (Esther 2:7)

3 Haman wanted to ____ the Jews (Esther 3:9-10)

4 "And let the ____ which pleaseth the king be queen" (Esther 2:4)

5 Because of Esther's courage, the law changed and "the Jews rested from their ____" (Esther 9:22)

48. THE WOMAN FOR THE HOUR — DECODER

	1	2	3	4	5
1	Y	N	I	U	C
2	P	T	D	J	R
3	E	K	W	G	M
4	V	B	O	S	F
5	L	Q	H	A	X

"45-43-25 13-45 11-43-14 32-31-31-21 52-14-13-31-22 54-22 22-53-13-44 22-13-35-31, 53-31-51-21 33-13-51-51 15-43-35-31 22-43 22-53-31 24-31-33-44 45-25-43-35 54-12-43-22-53-31-25 21-51-54-15-31. 42-14-22 11-43-14 54-12-23 11-43-14-25 45-54-22-53-31-25 ' 44 53-43-14-44-31 33-13-51-51 42-31 23-31-44-22-25-43-11-31-23. 33-53-43 32-12-43-33-44 13-45 11-43-14 53-54-41-31 12-43-22 42-31-15-43-35-31 52-14-31-31-12 45-43-25 44-14-15-53 54 22-13-35-31 54-44 22-53-13-44?"

Esther 4:14 NLV

THE BIBLE'S BOOK OF DANIEL: SHADRACH, MESHACH, AND ABED-NEGO IN THE FIERY FURNACE

Then Nebuchadnezzar was full of fury, and his facial expression was changed against Shadrach, Meshach, and Abed-nego. Therefore, he spoke and commanded that they should heat the furnace seven times more than it was usually heated. And he commanded the most mighty men who were in his army to bind Shadrach, Meshach, and Abed-nego and cast them into the burning fiery furnace.

DANIEL 3:19–20 SKJV

As a young man, Daniel—along with three others to be known as Shadrach, Meshach, and Abed-nego—are taken from their home in Jerusalem to serve the king of Babylon. Daniel's God-given ability to interpret dreams impresses King Nebuchadnezzar, whose vision of a huge statue, Daniel says, represents kingdoms of the world. Shadrach, Meshach, and Abed-nego find trouble when they disobey an order to bow before a statue of Nebuchadnezzar. As punishment, they are thrown into a fiery furnace, where they are protected by an angelic being the king says looks like the Son of God.

49. THE FIERY FURNACE — ACROSTIC

All Quotations NLV

How many men did the king see in the furnace? (Daniel 3:25) 1-24-10-28

The people were told to "____ the object of gold" (Daniel 3:5) 21-16-7-31-11-25-4

The king became ____ when the men disobeyed his order (Daniel 3:13) 15-3-23-19-8

"Their ____ were not burned" (Daniel 3:27) 9-32-26-17-2-29-12

"They did not even ____ like fire" (Daniel 3:27) 27-13-20-6-18

The king made the three men rulers in the ____ of Babylon (Daniel 3:30) 30-14-5-22

17-2-20 17-11-19-29-20 13-29-5 21-20-28-29 31-17-25-30-18 17-25-20-22 10-4 21-2-29-3 17-11-20-8 1-29-6-32 25-5-17-26 17-2-20 1-25-19-29.
DANIEL 3:23 NLV

50. GOD SHOWS NEBUCHADNEZZAR WHO'S BOSS — WORD SEARCH

S	H	A	D	R	A	C	H	E	S
K	A	G	E	T	S	A	W	S	E
B	M	V	N	F	T	W	H	I	R
T	E	A	E	I	O	K	O	A	V
W	S	C	N	R	V	N	U	R	A
A	H	V	D	G	O	R	S	P	N
L	A	N	M	I	E	D	E	L	T
R	C	B	T	M	O	L	S	S	S
F	H	A	Y	G	T	O	R	N	R
M	N	N	B	S	E	V	I	L	N

Nebuchadnezzar said, "**Praise** be to the **God** of **Shadrach**, Meshach, and Abed-nego. He has sent His **angel** and saved His **servants** who put their trust in Him. They changed the king's **word** and were ready to give up their **lives** instead of **serving** or worshiping any god except their own God. So I now make a **law** that if any people of any **nation** or language say anything against the God of Shadrach, **Meshach** and Abed-nego, they will be **torn** apart and their **houses** will be laid **waste**. For there is no other god who is able to **save** in this way."
DANIEL 3:28–29 NLV

THE BIBLE'S BOOK OF DANIEL: A NIGHT IN A LIONS' DEN

"My God sent His angel and shut the lions' mouths. They have not hurt me, because He knows that I am not guilty, and because I have done nothing wrong."

DANIEL 6:22 NLV

The next Babylonian king, Belshazzar, throws a drinking party using cups stolen from the temple in Jerusalem; he sees "the writing on the wall," which Daniel explains means Babylon will be taken over by the Medes. The Median king, Darius, respects Daniel and keeps him as an adviser. But other jealous officials try to hurt Daniel, who ends up in a den of lions. Once again, God protects His people—Daniel comes out without a scratch. Then his enemies are tossed into the den and mauled by the hungry lions. The last six chapters of Daniel describe the future, including the end of time.

51. DANIEL AND THE LIONS — CROSSWORD

All Quotations SKJV

Across

2 Daniel was thrown into the ____ of lions (Daniel 6:16)

4 In the morning, Daniel told King Darius, "They have not ____ me" (Daniel 6:21)

7 Darius told Daniel, "Your God, whom you serve continually, He will ____ you" (Daniel 6:17)

Down

1 Darius the Mede became king over Babylon after ____ was killed (Daniel 5:31)

3 Darius signed a ____ that no one could pray to anyone but the king (Daniel 6:7–9)

5 Daniel broke the law by praying to God ____ times each day (Daniel 6:13)

6 Darius declared that Daniel's God is "the ____ God" (Daniel 6:26)

52. DANIEL'S VISION OF THE END TIMES — DECODER

	1	2	3	4	5
1	G	B	V	O	J
2	D	Q	S	A	N
3	T	C	L	P	I
4	K	W	H	X	R
5	F	M	E	U	Y

"35 23-24-42 35-25 31-43-53 25-35-11-43-31 13-35-23-35-14-25-23 24-25-21, 12-53-43-14-33-21, 14-25-53 33-35-41-53 31-43-53 23-14-25 14-51 52-24-25 32-24-52-53 42-35-31-43 31-43-53 32-33-14-54-21-23 14-51 43-53-24-13-53-25 24-25-21 32-24-52-53 31-14 31-43-53 24-25-32-35-53-25-31 14-51 21-24-55-23, 24-25-21 31-43-53-55 12-45-14-54-11-43-31 43-35-52 25-53-24-45 12-53-51-14-45-53 43-35-52. 24-25-21 21-14-52-35-25-35-14-25 24-25-21 11-33-14-45-55 24-25-21 24 41-35-25-11-21-14-52 42-53-45-53 11-35-13-53-25 31-14 43-35-52, 31-43-24-31 24-33-33 34-53-14-34-33-53, 25-24-31-35-14-25-23, 24-25-21 33-24-25-11-54-24-11-53-23 23-43-14-54-33-21 23-53-45-13-53 43-35-52."

Daniel 7:13–14 SKJV

JONAH: DISOBEDIENT PROPHET OVERBOARD!

So they picked up Jonah and threw him into the sea, and the storm stopped. Then the men feared the Lord very much.

JONAH 1:15-16 NLV

God tells Jonah to preach in Nineveh, capital of the terrible Assyrian Empire. Jonah disobeys and sails in the opposite direction. A storm rocks Jonah's ship, and he goes overboard. Then Jonah spends three days in a giant fish's belly before deciding to obey God after all. When Jonah preaches, Nineveh turns from its sin—and God spares the city from destruction. Jonah wanted Nineveh to fall, and he pouts. The story ends with God saying He is concerned even for vicious unbelievers.

53. JONAH OVERBOARD — ACROSTIC

All Quotations NLV

Where Jonah was told to go (Jonah 1:2)	42-3-26-14-35-8-40
Where Jonah went to find a ship to run the other way (Jonah 1:3)	30-13-27-19-7
The sailors chose to draw _____ to figure out who was causing trouble (Jonah 1:7)	11-23-37-2-31
The sailors asked Jonah, "What is your _____?" (Jonah 1:8)	17-6-20-33-41-12-29
"The men were filled with _____" (Jonah 1:10)	4-36-25-18
"The wind was _____ even worse" (Jonah 1:13)	24-32-39-1-21-15-9
After the sailors threw Jonah into the sea, the storm _____ (Jonah 1:15)	38-10-34-28-5-22-16

10-40-22 32-34-18-16 38-36-15-41 25 24-21-9 4-3-31-40 10-39 38-1-23-32-32-6-1 30-13-33-7-40, 25-11-16 40-2 1-23-31 21-42 41-40-8 38-10-34-37-7-17-40 39-4 41-40-14 4-3-31-40 4-6-12 10-40-18-22-36 16-25-29-38 23-26-16 41-40-12-2-8 33-21-9-40-10-31.

JONAH 1:17 NLV

54. JONAH SHOULD HAVE CARED MORE FOR NINEVEH — WORD SEARCH

```
B V N I N E V E H Q
L W Z D R I G H T G
D O P L A N T P R L
M N L W I M E O D E
Y K L V O O W L R F
C T O V P R M M O T
A L I L M D K J L M
U T E C S H O U L D
S W F T H G I N K R
E S L A M I N A M G
```

The **Lord** said, "You had **loving**-pity on the **plant** which you did not **work** for. You did not **cause** it to **grow**. It came up during the **night** and died during the night. And **should** I not have loving-pity for **Nineveh**, the large **city** where more than 120,000 **people** live who do not **know** the difference between their **right** and **left** hand, as well as many **animals**?"

JONAH 4:10–11 NLV

THE BIBLE'S GOSPELS: THE BIRTH OF JESUS

The angel said to her, "Mary, do not be afraid. You have found favor with God. See! You are to become a mother and have a Son. You are to give Him the name Jesus. He will be great. He will be called the Son of the Most High."

Luke 1:30–32 NLV

The first four books of the New Testament are called the "Gospels." The word *gospel* means "good news," and these books share the good news of Jesus! The Gospels are Matthew, Mark, Luke, and John.

55. GOD SENDS AN ANGEL TO VISIT MARY — CROSSWORD

All Quotations KJV

Across

2 Mary was engaged to be married to this man (Luke 1:27)

4 The angel told Mary that she was ____ favoured (Luke 1:28)

7 The angel told Mary that she would have a son, and should "call his ____ Jesus" (Luke 1:31)

8 Mary said, "be it unto me according to thy ____" (Luke 1:38)

9 The angel said there would be no ____ to Jesus' kingdom (Luke 1:33)

Down

1 The angel told Mary, "The ____ Ghost shall come upon thee" (Luke 11:35)

3 Jesus would also be called the Son of the ____ (Luke 1:32)

5 The angel's name (Luke 1:26)

6 The angel said, "____ not, Mary" (Luke 1:30)

56. MARY IS EXPECTING A VERY SPECIAL BABY — DECODER

	1	2	3	4	5
1	F	C	P	U	K
2	I	W	R	E	M
3	X	D	V	Y	O
4	A	T	J	Q	G
5	N	H	S	L	B

42-52-24 55-21-23-42-52 35-11 43-24-53-14-53 12-52-23-21-53-42 22-41-53 54-21-15-24 42-52-21-53: 25-41-23-34 52-21-53 25-35-42-52-24-23 52-41-32 55-24-24-51 13-23-35-25-21-53-24-32 21-51 25-41-23-23-21-41-45-24 42-35 43-35-53-24-13-52. 55-24-11-35-23-24 42-52-24-34 22-24-23-24 25-41-23-23-21-24-32, 21-42 22-41-53 54-24-41-23-51-24-32 42-52-41-42 53-52-24 22-41-53 42-35 52-41-33-24 41 55-41-55-34 55-34 42-52-24 52-35-54-34 53-13-21-23-21-42. 43-35-53-24-13-52 . . . 42-52-35-14-45-52-42 21-42 22-35-14-54-32 55-24 45-35-35-32 42-35 55-23-24-41-15 42-52-24 13-23-35-25-21-53-24-32 25-41-23-23-21-41-45-24 22-21-42-52-35-14-42 13-24-35-13-54-24 15-51-35-22-21-51-45 21-42. 22-52-21-54-24 52-24 22-41-53 42-52-21-51-15-21-51-45 41-55-35-14-42 42-52-21-53, 41-51 41-51-45-24-54 35-11 42-52-24 54-35-23-32 12-41-25-24 42-35 52-21-25 21-51 41 32-23-24-41-25. 42-52-24 41-51-45-24-54 53-41-21-32, "43-35-53-24-13-52, 53-35-51 35-11 32-41-33-21-32, 32-35 51-35-42 55-24 41-11-23-41-21-32 42-35 42-41-15-24 25-41-23-34 41-53 34-35-14-23 22-21-11-24."

Matthew 1:18–20 NLV

THE BIBLE'S GOSPELS: MARY, JOSEPH, AND THE BABY JESUS

And she brought forth her firstborn son, and wrapped him in swaddling clothes, and laid him in a manger; because there was no room for them in the inn.

Luke 2:7 KJV

John's Gospel tells us, "In the beginning was the Word, and the Word was with God, and the Word was God" (John 1:1 KJV). Jesus is "the Word," and He is and always has been God—one member of "the Trinity," along with God the Father and the Holy Spirit. When Jesus came to earth to be born as a baby on the first Christmas, He had already existed forever as God. But now He was becoming a man like the people He had created.

57. MARY, JOSEPH, AND BABY JESUS — ACROSTIC

All Quotations SKJV

Mary and Joseph traveled to _____ (Luke 2:4) 27-33-42-2-2-24-19-30-11-26

Joseph was of the lineage of _____ (Luke 2:4) 37-13-32-4-43

Mary wrapped her baby in _____ clothes (Luke 2:7) 14-22-16-28-10-6-38-17-34

Mary laid baby Jesus in a _____ (Luke 2:7) 3-18-25-36-7-41

Shepherds were watching their _____ of sheep (Luke 2:8) 31-20-40-15-1

The heavenly host appeared _____ (Luke 2:13) 23-5-29-12-35-21-39-9

"31-40-41 42-40 9-40-5 38-23 27-40-41-21 42-2-4-14 12-13-9 38-25 42-2-35 15-4-42-9 40-31 29-16-32-38-10

18 23-13-32-4-40-41, 22-2-40 38-14 15-2-41-4-23-42 42-2-7 6-40-41-28."

LUKE 2:11 SKJV

58. THE VERY FIRST CHRISTMAS — WORD SEARCH

B	G	N	I	L	D	D	A	W	S
R	D	M	K	N	I	L	C	E	D
O	P	E	R	A	N	R	L	R	E
U	R	M	L	F	K	S	O	E	P
G	F	E	O	I	Y	P	T	H	P
H	C	R	G	A	V	L	H	T	A
T	T	H	D	N	N	E	S	L	R
H	R	O	O	M	A	O	R	L	W
S	H	O	U	L	D	M	S	E	M
N	R	O	B	T	S	R	I	F	D

And so it was, that while they were **there**, the **days** were accomplished that she **should** be **delivered**. And she **brought forth** her **firstborn son**, and **wrapped** Him in **swaddling cloths**, and **laid** Him in a **manger**, because there was no **room** for them in the **inn**.

LUKE 2:6–7 SKJV

THE BIBLE'S GOSPELS: SHEPHERDS LEARN OF THE BIRTH OF JESUS

In the same country there were shepherds in the fields. They were watching their flocks of sheep at night. The angel of the Lord came to them. The shining-greatness of the Lord shone around them. They were very much afraid.

Luke 2:8-9 NLV

The Gospel writer Luke was a Gentile—that means he was not part of God's "chosen people," the Jews. But Jesus came to save everyone, Jews and Gentiles both. So Luke's Gospel often shows God's love and concern for people whom others tended to overlook. Luke tells us that the first people to learn of Jesus' birth were poor, hardworking shepherds in the fields around Bethlehem!

59. CHRISTMAS SHEPHERDS — CROSSWORD

All Quotations KJV

Across

1 "For unto you is born this day in the city of ____ a Saviour, which is Christ the Lord" (Luke 2:11)

4 "Glory to God in the highest, and on earth ____, good will toward men" (Luke 2:14)

5 The shepherds would find the special baby lying in a ____ (Luke 2:12)

6 A large number; the "heavenly ____" (Luke 2:13)

8 What shined around the shepherds (Luke 2:9)

Down

2 When the shepherds saw the angel, they were "sore ____" (Luke 2:9)

3 The shepherds were "keeping ____ over their flock by night" (Luke 2:8)

4 The big group of angels was ____ God (Luke 2:13)

7 The angel brought "good tidings of great ____" (Luke 2:10)

60. SHEPHERDS SHARE THE GOOD NEWS — DECODER

	1	2	3	4	5
1	Y	M	D	X	Q
2	W	G	T	H	C
3	F	V	A	U	S
4	L	O	N	J	E
5	K	B	P	I	R

33-43-13 23-24-45-11 25-33-12-45 21-54-23-24 24-33-35-23-45 33-43-13

31-42-34-43-13 12-33-55-11 33-43-13 44-42-35-45-53-24, 33-43-13 23-24-45

52-33-52-11 41-11-54-43-22 54-43 33 12-33-43-22-45-55. 33-43-13 21-24-45-43

23-24-45-11 24-33-13 35-24-24-43 54-23, 23-24-45-11 21-54-13-45-41-11

12-33-13-45 51-43-42-21-43 23-24-45 35-33-11-54-43-22 23-24-33-23 21-33-35

23-42-41-13 23-24-45-12 25-42-43-25-45-55-43-54-43-22 23-24-54-35

25-24-54-41-13.

Luke 2:16–17 SKJV

THE BIBLE'S GOSPELS: YOUNG JESUS

And it came to pass that after three days they found Him in the temple, sitting in the midst of the teachers, both hearing them and asking them questions. And all who heard Him were astonished at His understanding and answers.

LUKE 2:46–47 SKJV

The four Gospels all tell about Jesus' life on earth. Matthew, Mark, Luke, and John have many of the same stories, but they sometimes tell something unique about Jesus. Only Matthew and Luke report Jesus' life between the time He was a baby and when He began His ministry as a man in His thirties. Matthew describes the visit of the wise men when Jesus was a toddler, and Luke shows Jesus as a twelve-year-old visiting the temple in Jerusalem.

61. THE VISIT OF THE WISE MEN — WORD SEARCH

And behold, the **star** that they saw in the **East** went before them, until it came and **stood** over where the **young Child** was. When they saw the star, they **rejoiced** with exceedingly **great** joy. And when they had come into the **house**, they saw the young Child with **Mary**, His **mother**, and **fell** down and worshipped Him. And when they had opened their **treasures**, they presented **gifts** to Him: **gold**, and frankincense, and **myrrh**.
MATTHEW 2:9–11 SKJV

S	R	M	T	A	E	R	G	G	P
T	Y	L	F	E	L	L	L	T	N
F	F	S	T	O	O	D	R	R	R
I	Y	S	T	M	Q	E	X	E	C
G	A	O	Y	Q	H	T	J	A	H
E	E	R	U	T	T	O	B	S	I
G	R	S	O	N	I	Y	R	U	L
H	O	M	U	C	G	R	A	R	D
R	L	L	E	O	Z	A	T	E	P
K	N	D	D	M	H	M	S	S	N

62. YOUNG JESUS IN THE TEMPLE — DECODER

	1	2	3	4	5
1	C	O	H	P	D
2	J	U	W	S	L
3	G	Y	A	Z	F
4	M	T	Q	V	K
5	E	R	I	N	B

33-54-15 23-13-51-54 13-51 23-33-24 42-23-51-25-44-51 32-51-33-52-24 12-25-15, 42-13-51-32 23-51-54-42 22-14 42-12 21-51-52-22-24-33-25-51-41 33-11-11-12-52-15-53-54-31 42-12 42-13-51 11-22-24-42-12-41 12-35 42-13-51 35-51-33-24-42. . . . 33-54-15 53-42 11-33-41-51 42-12 14-33-24-24 42-13-33-42 33-35-42-51-52 42-13-52-51-51 15-33-32-24 42-13-51-32 35-12-22-54-15 13-53-41 53-54 42-13-51 42-51-41-14-25-51, 24-53-42-42-53-54-31 53-54 42-13-51 41-53-15-24-42 12-35 42-13-51 42-51-33-11-13-51-52-24, 55-12-42-13 13-51-33-52-53-54-31 42-13-51-41 33-54-15 33-24-45-53-54-31 42-13-51-41 43-22-51-24-42-53-12-54-24. 33-54-15 33-25-25 23-13-12 13-51-33-52-15 13-53-41 23-51-52-51 33-24-42-12-54-53-24-13-51-15 33-42 13-53-24 22-54-15-51-52-24-42-33-54-15-53-54-31 33-54-15 33-54-24-23-51-52-24.
LUKE 2:42, 46–47 SKJV

THE BIBLE'S GOSPELS: JOHN BAPTIZES JESUS

Jesus came to the Jordan River from the town of Nazareth in the country of Galilee. He was baptized by John. As soon as Jesus came up out of the water, He saw heaven open up. The Holy Spirit came down on Him like a dove. A voice came from heaven and said, "You are My much-loved Son. I am very happy with You."

Mark 1:9–11 NLV

All four Gospels tell of the baptism of Jesus by His relative John. John was called "the Baptist" because he would dip people into the water of the Jordan River to show that they had repented of (or turned from) their sins. This was the beginning of Jesus' "public ministry" of preaching, teaching, and healing.

63. JOHN BAPTIZES JESUS — CROSSWORD

All Quotations NLV

Across

3 A voice from heaven said, "I am very ____ with" Jesus (Mark 1:11)

5 The Holy Spirit came down upon Jesus like a ____ (Mark 1:10)

6 John ate locusts and wild ____ (Mark 1:6)

8 Jesus met John at the ____ River (Mark 1:9)

Down

1 John's clothes were made from the hair of ____ (Mark 1:6)

2 John said he wasn't good enough to help Jesus remove His ____ (Mark 1:7)

4 "As soon as Jesus came up out of the water, He saw ____ open up" (Mark 1:10)

7 John said he baptized with water, but Jesus "will baptize you with the Holy ____" (Mark 1:8)

64. HOW JOHN THE BAPTIST DESCRIBED JESUS — DECODER

	1	2	3	4	5
1	G	B	P	Z	D
2	Y	I	R	F	N
3	L	W	H	U	K
4	X	C	V	T	M
5	E	O	J	A	S

44-33-51 25-51-41-44 15-54-21 53-52-33-25 44-33-51 12-54-13-44-22-55-44
55-54-32 53-51-55-34-55 42-52-45-22-25-11 44-52 33-22-45. 33-51 55-54-22-15,
"55-51-51! 44-33-51 31-54-45-12 52-24 11-52-15 32-33-52 44-54-35-51-55
54-32-54-21 44-33-51 55-22-25 52-24 44-33-51 32-52-23-31-15! 22 33-54-43-51
12-51-51-25 44-54-31-35-22-25-11 54-12-52-34-44 33-22-45. 22 55-54-22-15,
'52-25-51 22-55 42-52-45-22-25-11 54-24-44-51-23 45-51 32-33-52 22-55
45-52-23-51 22-45-13-52-23-44-54-25-44 44-33-54-25 22, 12-51-42-54-34-55-51 33-51 31-22-43-51-15
12-51-24-52-23-51 22 32-54-55 12-52-23-25.' 22 15-22-15 25-52-44 35-25-52-32 32-33-52 33-51 32-54-55,
12-34-44 22 33-54-43-51 42-52-45-51 44-52 12-54-13-44-22-14-51 32-22-44-33 32-54-44-51-23 55-52 44-33-51
53-51-32-55 45-22-11-33-44 35-25-52-32 54-12-52-34-44 33-22-45."

John 1:29–31 NLV

THE BIBLE'S GOSPELS: JESUS IS TEMPTED BY THE DEVIL

Jesus said to the devil, "Get away, Satan. It is written, 'You must worship the Lord your God. You must obey Him only.'"

MATTHEW 4:10 NLV

Matthew, Mark, and Luke all describe Jesus' temptation by the devil. Satan wanted Jesus to do something wrong—if Jesus would sin, then He couldn't save others from their sins. So the devil tempted Jesus to disobey God in some way. But for each of Satan's three temptations, Jesus quoted scripture and told the devil, "No." Then Jesus began choosing the twelve disciples who would follow Him and share the good news of the gospel.

65. JESUS IS TEMPTED IN THE WILDERNESS — ACROSTIC

All Quotations NLV

How many days and nights did Jesus go without food? (Matthew 4:2)	4-23-14-31-9
What did the devil tell Jesus to turn the stones into? (Matthew 4:3)	29-2-19-25-12
Jesus said, "Man is to ____ by every word that God speaks" (Matthew 4:4)	35-15-24-5
What is "The holy city"? (Matthew 4:5)	13-26-6-20-30-1-16-28-34
"You must not ____ the Lord your God" (Matthew 4:7)	21-10-7-32-18
"You must ____ the Lord your God" (Matthew 4:10)	33-8-17-27-11-3-22

13-10-30-20-27 33-25-30 16-28-12 29-9 18-11-26 11-8-35-9 27-32-3-17-15-21 31-23 1 12-5-30-19-6-18. 21-11-10-2-28 11-26 33-25-27 31-5-7-22-18-19-12 29-9 21-11-10 12-28-24-3-16.

MATTHEW 4:1 NLV

66. JESUS CALLS HIS FIRST DISCIPLES — WORD SEARCH

```
R A E S C O N C E H
C B R O T H E R S S
G S P G W T F E L I
N U E N B O A T G F
I S T K T S L N R L
O E E G A L I L E E
G J R N K K Z M O Q
V K H N L X Q L O F
Q O E A N D R E W N
J T W D H S E M A J
```

Jesus was **walking** by the Sea of **Galilee**. He saw two **brothers**. They were **Simon** (his other name was **Peter**) and **Andrew**, his brother. They were putting a **net** into the **sea** for they were fishermen. Jesus said to them, "**Follow** Me. I will make you **fish** for men!" At once they left their nets and followed Him. **Going** from there, Jesus saw two other brothers. They were **James** and **John**, the sons of Zebedee. They were sitting in a **boat** with their father, mending their nets. Jesus called them. At **once** they **left** the boat and their father and followed Jesus.

MATTHEW 4:18–22 NLV

THE BIBLE'S GOSPELS: JESUS' FIRST MIRACLE

Jesus said to the helpers, "Fill the jars with water." They filled them to the top.
Then He said, "Take some out and give it to the head man who is caring for the people."
They took some to him. The head man tasted the water that had become wine.

John 2:7–9 NLV

The Gospels of Matthew, Mark, and Luke are similar in many ways. But John's Gospel is quite different. John tells things about Jesus that the other Gospels don't—like the story of Jesus' very first miracle. At a wedding party in a town called Cana, Jesus turned water into wine. His amazing powers caused His disciples to put their trust in Him.

67. JESUS' FIRST MIRACLE — CROSSWORD

All Quotations KJV

Across

4 There was a wedding in ___ of Galilee (John 2:1)

5 Jesus and His ___ attended the wedding (John 2:2)

7 Jesus' ___ told Him the wine had run out (John 2:3)

8 "This ___ of miracles did Jesus" (John 2:11)

Down

1 "Thou hast kept the ___ wine until now" (John 2:10)

2 Jesus' disciples ___ on Him (John 2:11)

3 "Jesus saith unto them, Fill the waterpots with ___" (John 2:7)

6 What were the waterpots made of? (John 2:6)

68. JESUS IN THE TEMPLE — ACROSTIC

All Quotations NLV

It was time to remember the ___ leaving Egypt (John 2:13)	10-19-6-24
Jesus went to this city (John 2:13)	48-27-2-33-15-30-9-41-38
Men were ___ money in the temple (John 2:14)	20-45-11-42-16-4-34-28
Jesus made a ___ of small ropes (John 2:15)	7-21-35-17
Jesus pushed their ___ off the tables (John 2:15)	44-25-1-22-46
Jesus ___ the tables over (John 2:15)	31-12-43-39-8-47
Jesus called the temple "My ___ House" (John 2:16)	3-36-13-26-18-29 ' 49
This place was not for " ___ and selling," Jesus said (John 2:16)	23-14-32-37-5-40

31-45-19-39 21-4-24 3-25-9-9-25-6-27-29-15 2-41-38-22-44-23-8-43-18-47 31-26-30-31 35-31 7-11-49

6-29-37-31-31-19-42 4-34 31-45-27 45-25-9-32 7-2-35-31-37-1-16-24, "37 36-38 10-41-30-9-25-33-15 3-25-43

31-21-22 26-25-39-25-29 25-3 32-25-12-2 45-25-14-49-8."

JOHN 2:17 NLV

THE BIBLE'S GOSPELS: JESUS AND THE WOMAN AT THE WELL

A woman of Samaria came to get water. Jesus said to her, "Give Me a drink." His followers had gone to the town to buy food. The woman of Samaria said to Him, "You are a Jew. I am of Samaria. Why do You ask me for a drink when the Jews have nothing to do with the people of Samaria?"

JOHN 4:7–9 NLV

John is the only Gospel to tell the story of Jesus' talk with a woman at a well in Samaria. Jews and Samaritans were related, but didn't like each other. Jesus, though, came to save everyone, so He went to Samaria and asked a woman to give Him a drink. She was shocked by His request, and even more surprised when He told her things about her personal life. Jesus offered her "living water" (salvation), and she gladly accepted!

69. JESUS AND WOMAN AT THE WELL — WORD SEARCH

The **woman** said to Him, "I know the **Jews** are **looking** for **One** Who is **coming**. He is **called** the **Christ**. When He comes, He will **tell** us everything." **Jesus** said to her, "I am the Christ, the One **talking** with you!" . . . The woman left her **water** jar and went into the **town**. She said to the men, "Come and see a **Man** Who told me **everything** I ever did! Can this be the Christ?" They went out of town and **came** to Him.
JOHN 4:25–26, 28–30 NLV

G	T	S	I	R	H	C	P	Y	L
W	A	T	E	R	A	S	L	D	Z
C	T	N	K	L	X	U	D	T	N
O	A	C	L	G	S	S	J	A	A
M	O	E	A	W	C	E	D	L	M
I	D	N	E	M	M	J	V	K	O
N	L	J	E	L	E	C	T	I	W
G	N	L	L	O	O	K	I	N	G
L	Y	X	E	N	W	O	T	G	L
G	N	I	H	T	Y	R	E	V	E

70. SAMARITANS FOLLOW JESUS — DECODER

	1	2	3	4	5
1	H	A	U	K	E
2	J	T	S	O	C
3	M	Y	G	W	V
4	R	F	Q	N	I
5	D	X	L	P	B

31-12-44-32 54-15-24-54-53-15 45-44 22-11-12-22 22-24-34-44 24-42 23-12-31-12-41-45-12 . . . 23-12-45-51 22-24 22-11-15 34-24-31-12-44, "44-24-34 34-15 55-15-53-45-15-35-15-! 45-22 45-23 44-24 53-24-44-33-15-41 55-15-25-12-13-23-15 24-42 34-11-12-22 32-24-13 23-12-45-51 12-55-24-13-22 21-15-23-13-23 55-13-22 34-15 11-12-35-15 11-15-12-41-51 11-45-31 24-13-41-23-15-53-35-15-23. 34-15 14-44-24-34, 42-24-41 23-13-41-15, 22-11-12-22 11-15 45-23 22-11-15 25-11-41-45-23-22, 22-11-15 24-44-15 34-11-24 23-12-35-15-23 31-15-44 24-42 22-11-45-23 34-24-41-53-51 42-41-24-31 22-11-15 54-13-44-45-23-11-31-15-44-22 24-42 22-11-15-45-41 23-45-44-23."
JOHN 4:39, 42 NLV

THE BIBLE'S GOSPELS: JESUS HEALS THE SICK

And when Jesus had entered into Capernaum, a centurion came to Him, beseeching Him and saying, "Lord, my servant is lying at home paralyzed, grievously tormented." And Jesus said to him, "I will come and heal him."

MATTHEW 8:5–7 SKJV

The Gospel writers told many stories of Jesus healing blind and lame people, casting out demons from the possessed, and even raising people from the dead! Matthew told back-to-back stories of Jesus healing a man with a skin disease called leprosy, and also the very ill servant of a Roman army commander called a centurion.

71. JESUS AND THE LEPER — WORD SEARCH

T	O	U	C	H	E	D	L	K	T
S	F	L	L	I	W	E	B	C	N
U	B	O	M	E	P	P	N	L	W
S	E	Z	L	E	P	I	B	E	O
E	H	N	R	L	A	R	Q	A	D
J	O	C	A	T	O	C	O	N	D
M	L	N	N	E	L	W	A	S	X
G	D	U	P	W	L	H	E	E	Y
J	O	R	F	K	T	C	K	D	T
M	U	L	T	I	T	U	D	E	S

When He had come **down** from the **mountain**, great **multitudes followed** Him. And **behold**, a **leper** came and worshipped Him, saying, "Lord, if You **will**, You can make me **clean**." And **Jesus** put out His **hand** and **touched** him, saying, "I will; be clean." And immediately his **leprosy** was **cleansed**.
MATTHEW 8:1–3 SKJV

72. JESUS AND THE CENTURION — CROSSWORD

All Quotations SKJV

Across

1 Town where the centurion worked (Matthew 8:5)

3 The captain said, "Lord, I am not ____ that You should come under my roof" (Matthew 8:8)

6 Jesus told the centurion, "As you have ____, so let it be done for you" (Matthew 8:13)

7 "His servant was healed in the very same ____" (Matthew 8:13)

Down

2 The centurion's servant was ____ (Matthew 8:6)

4 The centurion asked Jesus to "only speak the ____" to heal his servant (Matthew 8:8)

5 Jesus had not "found such great ____" in all Israel (Matthew 8:10)

THE BIBLE'S GOSPELS: JESUS CALMS A STORM

And He arose and rebuked the wind and said to the sea, "Peace, be still." And the wind ceased and there was a great calm. And He said to them, "Why are you so fearful? How is it that you have no faith?"

MARK 4:39–40 SKJV

The Gospels of Matthew, Mark, and Luke all tell the story of Jesus calming a storm on the Sea of Galilee. Since He created the world, Jesus has power over the forces of nature—and by His simple command, "Be quiet! Be still," a wild storm immediately stopped. When Jesus and His disciples landed, they met a man who was full of demons. Jesus ordered them to leave the poor man. Just like the storm, the demons had to obey Jesus' power and authority!

73. JESUS CALMS THE STORMY SEA — ACROSTIC

All Quotations NLV

What time of day was it? (Mark 4:35)	41-5-38-22-14-35-29
Jesus and His disciples got into a _____ (Mark 4:36)	37-15-1-26
"A bad wind ______ came up" (Mark 4:37)	23-12-20-6-30
What did the disciples call Jesus? (Mark 4:38)	39-9-16-27-3-40-33
Jesus spoke sharp _____ to the wind (Mark 4:39)	17-31-7-10-24
"Be _____! Be still," Jesus said to the sea (Mark 4:39)	28-2-18-34-13
Jesus' first question was, "_____ are you so full of fear?" (Mark 4:40)	32-11-21
Jesus then asked, "Do you not have _____?" (Mark 4:40)	4-25-19-36-8

36-8-34-21 32-40-7-9 5-38-33-21 30-2-27-11 25-4-6-16-19-10 1-35-10 24-25-18-10 13-31 41-16-27-3 20-39-8-34-7,

"17-11-15 14-23 12-3-19-24? 40-5-9-22 26-8-38 32-18-35-10 1-22-10 17-25-5-38-23 31-37-41-21 11-14-30!"

MARK 4:41 NLV

74. JESUS HEALS A DEMON-POSSESSED MAN — WORD SEARCH

```
D N A M M O C T E D
Y E K A L L D M P E
L E G I O N A R E K
T R L B D N Y A E O
N K K E S E G L T H
E D E G U N M L S C
L P L G S I K O K H
O W G E E W Z W N L
I T G D J S X T D S
V H N I A T N U O M
```

And **Jesus** asked him, saying, "What is your **name**?" And he said, "**Legion**," because many **demons** had entered into him. And they **begged** Him that He would not **command** them to go out into the **deep**. And there was a **herd** of many **swine** feeding on the **mountain**. And they begged Him that He would **allow** them to enter into them. And He allowed them. Then the demons went out of the man and entered into the swine, and the herd ran **violently** down a **steep** place into the **lake** and were **choked**.

LUKE 8:30–33 SKJV

THE BIBLE'S GOSPELS: JESUS FEEDS FIVE THOUSAND WITH A YOUNG BOY'S LUNCH

Then He took the five loaves and the two fish, and looking up to heaven, He blessed them, and broke them, and gave to the disciples to set before the multitude. And they ate and were all filled, and twelve baskets of fragments that remained were taken up by them.

LUKE 9:16–17 SKJV

Only two of Jesus' miracles are reported in all four Gospels—His resurrection from the dead and His feeding of five thousand men (plus women and children) from one boy's lunch of five small loaves of bread and two fish. Shortly afterward, Peter realized exactly who Jesus was—God's Messiah, the Christ, the one Savior for the whole world.

75. THE BREAD AND THE FISH — CROSSWORD

Luke 9 SKJV

Across

2 How many fish did the disciples find? (Luke 9:13)

3 Jesus was teaching the crowd about "the ____ of God" (Luke 9:11)

5 Jesus had told the disciples, "You give them something to ____" (Luke 9:13)

6 Looking up to heaven, Jesus ____ the loaves and fish (Luke 9:16)

8 How many baskets of leftover food were there? (Luke 9:17)

Down

1 The disciples wanted Jesus to ____ the multitude away (Luke 9:12)

2 "There were about five ____ men" (Luke 9:14)

4 How many loaves of bread did the disciples find? (Luke 9:13)

7 Jesus and the disciples made the crowd ____ down (Luke 9:15)

76. PETER UNDERSTANDS WHO JESUS IS — DECODER

	1	2	3	4	5
1	W	F	R	I	L
2	N	Z	Y	B	P
3	A	X	E	T	G
4	V	M	S	O	D
5	K	U	C	H	J

11-54-14-15-33 55-33-43-52-43 11-31-43 25-13-31-23-14-21-35 31-15-44-21-33, 54-14-43 12-44-15-15-44-11-33-13-43 11-33-13-33 11-14-34-54 54-14-42. 55-33-43-52-43 31-43-51-33-45 34-54-33-42, "11-54-44 45-44 25-33-44-25-15-33 43-31-23 34-54-31-34 14 31-42?" 34-54-33-23 43-31-14-45, "55-44-54-21 34-54-33 24-31-25-34-14-43-34, 24-52-34 43-44-42-33 43-31-23 33-15-14-55-31-54. 44-34-54-33-13-43 43-31-23 34-54-31-34 44-21-33 44-12 34-54-33 33-31-13-15-23 25-13-33-31-53-54-33-13-43 54-31-43 24-33-33-21 13-31-14-43-33-45 12-13-44-42 34-54-33 45-33-31-45." 55-33-43-52-43 43-31-14-45 34-44 34-54-33-42, "24-52-34 11-54-44 45-44 23-44-52 43-31-23 34-54-31-34 14 31-42?" 25-33-34-3313 43-31-14-45, "23-44-52 31-13-33 34-54-33 53-54-13-14-43-34 44-12 35-44-45."
LUKE 9:18–20 NLV

THE BIBLE'S GOSPELS:
PETER (BRIEFLY) WALKS ON WATER TO JESUS

But when he saw the wind was boisterous, he was afraid. And beginning to sink, he cried, saying, "Lord, save me!"

MATTHEW 14:30 SKJV

The Gospels of Matthew, Mark, and John all describe Jesus miraculously walking on the water of the Sea of Galilee. But only Matthew shows *Peter* doing the same thing—very briefly. When Jesus walked on the water to His disciples during a wild storm on the lake, Peter asked if he could join Jesus. The Lord said, "Come!" and Peter walked on water too. . .until he got distracted by the storm.

77. PETER SINKS IN THE SEA — ACROSTIC

All Quotations SKJV

Clue	Code
The ship was "tossed with ______" (Matthew 14:24)	21-5-30-25-13
"The wind was ______" (Matthew 14:24)	33-43-2-35-24-18-39-9
Who walked on the water first? (Matthew 14:25)	44-12-7-37-22
It was the "_____ watch of the night" (Matthew 14:25)	26-19-34-14-6-42
Who saw Jesus walking on the sea? (Matthew 14:26)	29-10-1-40-23-31-17-38-46
The command Jesus said to Peter (Matthew 14:29)	3-27-15-45
"_______ to sink," Peter cried out for Jesus to save him (Matthew 14:30)	16-36-8-41-32-4-20-11-28

18-11-29 20-15-15-36-29-41-5-6-45-17-9 44-38-46-34-1 22-35-14-12-6-33-42-25-29 27-34-35 42-23-7 42-18-4-29 5-32-29 3-18-34-8-42-6 42-10-15, 5-2-29 13-18-20-29 35-43 42-41-15, "27 9-43-34 27-26 17-23-6-35-17-36 26-5-10-6-42, 21-42-9 29-20-29 9-43-34 29-27-34-16-35?"

Matthew 14:31 SKJV

78. "TRULY YOU ARE THE SON OF GOD" — WORD SEARCH

```
W O R S H I P P E D
T D H A N D W I N D
T B T C S G N R E G
D S U N A P N H Y O
E U P O I U C K L D
S S S H D T G I U E
A E S O E L T H R M
E J P R N T G N T A
C W T T L J L R D C
F S Q E H T I A F C
```

And immediately **Jesus stretched** out His **hand** and **caught** him, and **said** to him, "O you of **little faith**, why did you **doubt**?" And when they **came** into the **ship**, the **wind ceased**. Then those who were in the ship came and **worshipped** Him, saying, "**Truly** You are the **Son** of **God**."

Matthew 14:31–33 SKJV

THE BIBLE'S GOSPELS: JESUS SHOWS HIS GLORY

Six days later Jesus took Peter and James and John with Him. He led them up to a high mountain by themselves. Jesus was changed as they looked at Him. His clothes did shine. They were as white as snow. No one on earth could clean them so white.

MARK 9:2–3 NLV

Three Gospel writers tell about Jesus' *transfiguration*—a big word that means "change." Matthew, Mark, and Luke all describe the day Jesus took a few disciples up on a mountain, where He began to glow with a bright white light. Peter, James, and John all got a glimpse of Jesus' glory as God—and it scared them! Then they heard God the Father's voice from heaven, saying "This is My much-loved Son. Listen to Him" (Mark 9:7 NLV).

79. THE TRANSFIGURATION — DECODER

22-14-44-25-33 24-55-43-11-33 54-22-41-52 22-31-33-24-13 42-24-52-25-52

11-22-54 52-22-55-54 33-11-24-52-24 33-11-55-53-43-52, 11-24 33-44-44-15

32-24-33-24-13 22-53-54 42-22-23-24-52 22-53-54 42-44-11-53 45-55-33-11

11-55-23. 33-11-24-41 45-24-53-33 25-32 44-53 22 23-44-25-53-33-22-55-53

33-44 32-13-22-41. 22-52 42-24-52-25-52 32-13-22-41-24-54, 11-24 45-22-52

35-11-22-53-43-24-54 55-53 51-44-44-15-52 14-24-31-44-13-24 33-11-24-23.

11-55-52 35-51-44-33-11-24-52 14-24-35-22-23-24 45-11-55-33-24 22-53-54 52-11-55-53-55-53-43 14-13-55-43-11-33.

LUKE 9:28–29 NLV

	1	2	3	4	5
1	H	V	R	B	K
2	X	A	M	E	U
3	F	P	T	Q	C
4	Y	J	G	O	W
5	L	S	N	D	I

80. JESUS, MOSES, AND ELIJAH — WORD SEARCH

```
G N I N I H S P C V
D S O O N J D T L S
E N H T A E D R O U
K H H T Y W V L T S
L A B A H L J A H E
A P R I L G O F E J
T P T J J N I O S H
J E M O S E S R K M
C N H A J I L E B S
Q X C H A N G E D D
```

As **Jesus prayed**, He was **changed** in **looks** before them. His **clothes** became **white** and **shining bright**. Two men **talked** with Jesus. They were **Moses** and **Elijah**. They looked like the shining-greatness of **heaven** as they talked about His **death** in Jerusalem which was **soon** to **happen**.

LUKE 9:29–31 NLV

THE BIBLE'S GOSPELS: JESUS WELCOMES THE CHILDREN

Jesus took a little child and put him among them. He said, "For sure, I tell you, unless you have a change of heart and become like a little child, you will not get into the holy nation of heaven."

MATTHEW 18:2–3 NLV

The Gospels show that Jesus loves children. He scolded His disciples for trying to keep little ones away from Him. He put His hands on the children and blessed them. And He made little children the example of the kind of people who can be saved and go to heaven—they are simple and trusting!

81. JESUS AND THE CHILDREN — ACROSTIC

All Quotations SKJV

People brought their _____ to Jesus (Mark 10:13)	2-30-21-37-8-33-28-19
Jesus' disciples _____ the people (Mark 10:13)	15-25-12-20-34-18-5
Jesus was _____ with the disciples' behavior (Mark 10:14)	27-11-4-13-10-31-24-35-6-1
"Allow the _____ children to come to me," Jesus said (Mark 10:14)	38-9-22-16-32-26
". . .of such is the _____ of God" (Mark 10:14)	7-14-29-3-17-23-36

24-19-17 30-26 16-23-23-7 22-30-6-36 20-13 9-19 30-14-35 24-33-36-4, 13-20-16 30-21-35 30-24-19-8-4 23-19
22-30-31-36, 24-19-5 12-10-18-35-4-25-1 16-30-28-36.
MARK 10:16 SKJV

82. RECEIVE THE KINGDOM OF GOD LIKE A LITTLE CHILD — WORD SEARCH

T	O	U	C	H	L	D	R	S	N
D	Z	E	R	C	J	E	T	R	E
R	I	W	M	E	T	N	H	E	R
E	J	S	S	O	A	T	G	B	D
C	J	U	C	F	C	E	U	U	L
E	S	B	N	I	K	R	O	K	I
I	D	I	K	R	P	M	R	E	H
V	W	O	L	L	A	L	B	D	C
E	M	Y	L	U	R	T	E	M	V
B	K	I	N	G	D	O	M	S	W

And they also **brought infants** to Him, that He would **touch** them. But when His **disciples** saw it, they **rebuked** them. But **Jesus** called them to Him and said, "**Allow** little **children** to **come** to Me, and do not forbid them, for of such is the **kingdom** of God. **Truly** I say to you, whoever shall not **receive** the kingdom of God as a little child shall in no way **enter** it."
LUKE 18:15–17 SKJV

THE BIBLE'S GOSPELS: JESUS' "TRIUMPHAL ENTRY" INTO JERUSALEM

Many people put their clothes down on the road. Others cut branches off the trees and put them down on the road. Those who went in front and those who followed spoke with loud voices, "Greatest One! Great and honored is He Who comes in the name of the Lord!"

MARK 11:8–9 NLV

When all four Gospel writers tell about an event in Jesus' life, it must be important! Matthew, Mark, Luke, and John all describe the "triumphal entry," the day Jesus rode a young donkey into Jerusalem to the cheers of the people. It was an exciting time and a fulfillment of a prophecy from hundreds of years earlier: "Be full of joy, O people of Zion! Call out in a loud voice, O people of Jerusalem! See, your King is coming to you. He is fair and good and has the power to save. He is not proud and sits on a donkey, on the son of a female donkey" (Zechariah 9:9 NLV).

83. THE TRIUMPHAL ENTRY — CROSSWORD

All Quotations SKJV

Across

1 Some people cut ____ off trees and laid them on the road (Mark 11:8)

4 What did the disciples lay on the colt? (Mark 11:7)

7 Where were the disciples to find the colt Jesus rode on? (Mark 11:2)

8 What city was Jesus entering? (Mark 11:11)

Down

2 The word of praise people shouted to Jesus (Mark 11:9)

3 Jesus ____ on the colt (Mark 11:7)

5 Some people "spread their garments on the ____" (Mark 11:8)

6 Jesus had been with His disciples at the Mount of ____ (Mark 11:1)

84. JESUS THE PROPHET FROM NAZARETH — DECODER

	1	2	3	4	5
1	N	C	W	M	O
2	F	Y	R	G	D
3	X	I	B	V	S
4	E	L	U	J	Z
5	K	P	H	T	A

55-11-25 13-53-41-11 53-41 53-55-25 12-15-14-41 32-11-54-15 44-41-23-43-35-55-42-41-14, 55-42-42 54-53-41 12-32-54-22 13-55-35 14-15-34-41-25, 35-55-22-32-11-24, "13-53-15 32-35 54-53-32-35?" 55-11-25 54-53-41 14-43-42-54-32-54-43-25-41 35-55-32-25, "54-53-32-35 32-35 44-41-35-43-35 54-53-41 52-23-15-52-53-41-54 21-23-15-14 11-55-45-55-23-41-54-53 15-21 24-55-42-32-42-41-41."

MATTHEW 21:10–11 SKJV

THE BIBLE'S GOSPELS: JUDAS BETRAYS JESUS WITH A KISS

Now he who betrayed Him gave them a sign, saying, "Whomever I kiss, that same is He. Hold Him fast." And immediately he came to Jesus and said, "Hail, Master," and kissed Him.

MATTHEW 26:48–49 SKJV

Judas Iscariot is the bad guy of Jesus' story, and all four Gospels tell of his terrible betrayal of Jesus. It was Judas—one of the twelve disciples—who led enemies to arrest Jesus in the garden of Gethsemane. Jesus knew that Judas would betray Him, and God used Judas' bad choice to bring about the plan of salvation. But Judas, who should have known better, destroyed his own life.

85. JESUS BETRAYED — ACROSTIC

All Quotations NLV

Judas ____ was one of Jesus' followers, or disciples (Matthew 26:14) 28-10-42-30-18-37-22-4

Judas met with the ____ leaders (Matthew 26:14) 21-5-33-41-13-39-9-25-17

Judas was paid thirty pieces of ____ (Matthew 26:15) 44-24-16-1-20-36

____ was sitting with His followers (Matthew 26:20) 2-27-14-31-40

How many followers were there? (Matthew 26:20) 38-7-23-34-11-43

Jesus said, "One of you will ____ Me over" (Matthew 26:21) 15-32-3-26

Each one asked, "____, is it I?" (Matthew 26:22) 35-6-29-12

At the meal, Jesus said, "Take, eat, this is ____ body" (Matthew 26:26) 19-8

2-25-12-32-40 7-30-14 38-15-43 6-3-23 7-15-9 7-32-40 15-30-3-26-24-3-13 2-23-17-25-10 22-1-27-29.

15-20 40-30-39-12, "4-5-32-42-15-43-36, 30-19 41 38-15-23 6-3-27?" 2-5-14-25-44 17-32-37-26 38-22 15-28-19,

"8-9-31 15-30-1-20 10-32-28-12 24-4."

MATTHEW 26:25 NLV

86. JUDAS' SAD ENDING — WORD SEARCH

K	T	V	S	R	E	D	A	E	L
D	O	I	N	G	J	Y	P	K	G
Y	E	N	O	M	R	E	F	H	L
K	T	H	I	R	T	Y	S	O	Z
I	P	H	O	P	S	G	S	U	N
L	I	S	R	I	A	N	I	S	S
L	E	B	L	G	D	O	N	E	V
E	C	V	G	W	U	R	N	D	D
D	E	P	O	R	J	W	E	K	B
R	S	T	X	H	A	N	D	E	D

Then **Judas** was **sorry** he had **handed** Jesus over when he saw that **Jesus** was going to be **killed**. He took back the **thirty pieces** of **silver** and gave it to the head religious **leaders** and the other leaders. He said, "I have **sinned** because I handed over a Man Who has done no **wrong**." And they said, "What is that to us? That is your own **doing**." He threw the **money** down in the **house** of God and went outside. Then he went away and killed himself by hanging from a **rope**.

MATTHEW 27:3–5 NLV

THE BIBLE'S GOSPELS: JESUS DIES ON A CROSS

It was dark over all the earth from noon until three o'clock. The sun did not shine. . . . Then Jesus cried out with a loud voice, "Father, into Your hands I give My spirit." When He said this, He died.

LUKE 23:44-46 NLV

The Gospels all build up to the moment when Jesus died on the cross for people's sins. That is what He came to earth for! The perfect man paid the price for every human sin ever committed. And if we tell Him we are sorry for our sins, His death will cover the punishment for all the wrong we've ever done!

87. JESUS ON THE CROSS — CROSSWORD

All Quotations SKJV

Across

2 It means "killed on a cross" (John 19:16)

3 Who gambled for Jesus' garments? (John 19:23)

4 Jesus' final words were, "It is ____" (John 19:30)

7 The Hebrew name for the place where Jesus died (John 19:17)

Down

1 A sign on the cross said, "Jesus of Nazareth the King of the ____" (John 19:19)

3 "He bowed His head and gave up the ____" (John 19:30)

5 Jesus was killed at "The Place of a ____" (John 19:17)

6 How many others were crucified with Jesus? (John 19:18)

88. JESUS IS BURIED — DECODER

	1	2	3	4	5
1	B	Q	J	P	E
2	G	X	T	F	K
3	L	V	I	U	A
4	S	C	Y	O	N
5	M	R	H	W	D

23-53-15-45 23-53-15-43 23-44-44-25 23-53-15 11-44-55-43 44-24 13-15-41-34-41 54-33-23-53 23-53-15 41-14-33-42-15-41 35-45-55 14-34-23 33-23 33-45 31-33-45-15-45 42-31-44-23-53-41. 23-53-33-41 54-35-41 23-53-15 54-35-43 23-53-15 13-15-54-41 51-35-55-15 35 11-44-55-43 52-15-35-55-43 24-44-52 23-53-15 21-52-35-32-15. 23-53-15-52-15 54-35-41 35 21-35-52-55-15-45 45-15-35-52 23-53-15 14-31-35-42-15 54-53-15-52-15 53-15 53-35-55 11-15-15-45 45-35-33-31-15-55 23-44 23-53-15 42-52-44-41-41. 33-45 23-53-15 21-35-52-55-15-45 23-53-15-52-15 54-35-41 35 45-15-54 21-52-35-32-15 33-45 23-53-15 41-33-55-15 44-24 23-53-15 53-33-31-31. 45-44 44-45-15 53-35-55 15-32-15-52 11-15-15-45 31-35-33-55 23-53-15-52-15.

John 19:40–41 NLV

THE BIBLE'S GOSPELS AND BOOK OF ACTS: JESUS RETURNS TO LIFE. . .AND THEN TO HEAVEN

And He led them out as far as to Bethany, and He lifted up His hands and blessed them. And it came to pass, while He blessed them, He was parted from them and was carried up into heaven.

LUKE 24:50–51 SKJV

Luke, who wrote the third Gospel and the book of Acts, provides many details of Jesus' ascension. To "ascend" is to go up—and the word ascension describes Jesus' rising up into heaven. When Jesus came back to life after the crucifixion, He proved His power over death. Forty days later, He ascended into heaven, where He is right now preparing a place for His followers!

89. AFTER THE RESURRECTION — ACROSTIC

All Quotations SKJV

After His resurrection, Jesus asked the disciples, "_____ you any food here?" (Luke 24:41) 27-18-31-6

". . .it was necessary for _____ to suffer and to rise" (Luke 24:46) 3-41-16-22-10-49

"I send the promise of My _____ on you" (Luke 24:49) 25-12-44-32-1-19

The town Jesus led the disciples to (Luke 24:50) 34-42-7-37-23-30-13

"He lifted up His hands and _____ them" (Luke 24:50) 29-14-38-20-46-4-36

What the disciples did to Jesus (Luke 24:52) 48-2-33-24-43-8-39-47-15-45

The disciples "returned to _____ with great joy" (Luke 24:52) 11-28-40-5-21-35-17-9-26

35-30-45 8-7 3-23-26-9 44-2 47-12-21-24, 48-43-22-17-28 37-15 29-14-4-46-20-38-36 49-32-42-26,

41-1 48-18-10 39-35-40-7-6-45 25-33-2-26 44-27-9-26 23-30-36 48-12-46 3-18-16-40-8-28-45 5-47 22-30-49-2

43-15-35-31-4-30.

LUKE 24:51 SKJV

90. JESUS' ASCENSION — WORD SEARCH

```
Q G A L I L E E Q P
N C L O U D R F H R
J B N O Y H Q E A D
E G E K G S A L E N
S N K E X V I H C E
U I O D E M C G C K
S Z P N I T V O H A
W A S S A J M L N T
R G T W K E T I H W
```

And when He had **spoken** these things, while they **watched**, He was taken up, and a **cloud** received Him out of their **sight**. And while they **looked** steadfastly toward **heaven** as He went up, behold, two men stood by them in **white** apparel, who also said, "Men of **Galilee**, why do you stand **gazing** up into heaven? This same **Jesus**, who has been **taken** up from you to heaven, shall so **come** in **similar** manner as you have seen Him go into heaven."
ACTS 1:9–11 SKJV

THE BIBLE'S BOOK OF ACTS: THE HOLY SPIRIT COMES TO LIVE INSIDE BELIEVERS

All at once there was a sound from heaven like a powerful wind. It filled the house where they were sitting. Then they saw tongues which were divided that looked like fire. These came down on each one of them. They were all filled with the Holy Spirit.

Acts 2:2-4 NLV

Officially called "Acts of the Apostles," the book of Acts is a bridge between the story of Jesus in the Gospels and the life of the church in the letters that follow. Luke begins with Jesus' ascension into heaven forty days after the resurrection. Ten days later, God sends the Holy Spirit on the festival day of Pentecost—and the church is born. Through the Spirit, the disciples gain power to preach boldly about Jesus, and three thousand people become Christians that day.

91. THE DAY OF PENTECOST — CROSSWORD

All Quotations SKJV

Across

2 The believers were filled with the ____ Spirit (Acts 2:4)

4 Some made fun and said the believers were "full of new ____" (Acts 2:13)

5 "Every man heard them ____ in his own language" (Acts 2:6)

7 Everyone was ____ by what had happened (Acts 2:12)

8 "And there were ____ Jews dwelling in Jerusalem" (Acts 2:5)

Down

1 People were talking about the "wonderful ____ of God" (Acts 2:11)

2 An unusual sound filled the ____ (Acts 2:2)

3 Tongues of ____ rested on each of the believers (Acts 2:3)

4 The believers heard a sound like a "mighty rushing ___" (Acts 2:2)

6 The believers were all in one ____ (Acts 2:1)

1		2							3
						4			
5	6								
	7								
8									

92. WHAT REALLY HAPPENED AT PENTECOST — WORD SEARCH

D O G P R O P H E T
G N U O Y N M M H D
M V D D E D T S T A
V J A K K D E S I U
T Y O Z R L H N R G
S P L E F T C O I H
S Y A R L R I I P T
C M S P U N H S S E
S D T K M O W I W R
S O N S H Y P V H S

This is that **which** was **spoken** by the **prophet Joel**; And it shall come to pass in the **last days**, saith **God**, I will **pour** out of my **Spirit** upon all **flesh**: and your **sons** and your **daughters** shall prophesy, and your **young** men shall see **visions**, and your old men shall dream **dreams**.
Acts 2:16–17 KJV

THE BIBLE'S BOOK OF ACTS:
PHILIP WITNESSES TO A MAN FROM ETHIOPIA

Philip ran up to him. He saw that the man from Ethiopia was reading from the writings of the early preacher Isaiah and said, "Do you understand what you are reading?" The man from Ethiopia said, "How can I, unless someone teaches me?"

ACTS 8:30–31 NLV

The book of Acts shows how the good news about Jesus spread to all people. At first, the followers of Jesus lived mainly around Jerusalem. But then enemies of Jesus started persecuting believers, making their lives hard. One man, Stephen, was killed for following Jesus. Believers scattered to other places, telling people about Jesus wherever they went. Some even became missionaries, people who went out specifically to share the good news. Philip was an early "evangelist," someone who preaches salvation through Jesus. He helped a man from Ethiopia to be saved.

93. CHRISTIANS SCATTER AND SHARE JESUS — WORD SEARCH

Saul thought it was all right that **Stephen** was **killed**. On that day people started to work very **hard** against the **church** in Jerusalem. All the **followers**, except the missionaries, were made to **leave**. They went to parts of the countries of **Judea** and **Samaria**. Good men put Stephen in a **grave**. There was much **sorrow** because of him. During this time Saul was making it very hard for the church. He went into every **house** of the followers of **Jesus** and took men and women and put them in **prison**. Those who had been made to go to other places preached the **Word** as they went.
Acts 8:1–4 NLV

```
K I L L E D L L K T
F N V Z A E D U J D
Y O D H K L N A V W
A S L N A E T S O L
J I Q L H R W R E C
E R R P O O D A V H
S P E A R W V L A U
U T Z R M E E M R R
S L O Y W A Z R G C
X S F H O U S E S H
```

94. PHILIP AND THE ETHIOPIAN EUNUCH — ACROSTIC

All Quotations SKJV

"And the angel of the _____ spoke to Philip" (Acts 8:26)	4-23-15-43
The eunuch had "great _____" (Acts 8:27)	38-16-20-41-35-24-7-45-12
What the eunuch came to Jerusalem to do (Acts 8:27)	32-1-25-30-17-9-42
The _____ spoke to Philip (Acts 8:29)	44-28-6-14-36-22
". . .like a ____ before its shearer is silent" (Acts 8:32)	13-33-26-2
"he went on his way _____" (Acts 8:39)	21-8-37-18-10-29-5-34-39
Where Philip was found after he disappeared (Acts 8:40)	40-3-27-31-11-19

40-34-43 17-8 29-27-26-26-33-34-43-8-43 31-41-8 29-17-38-14-5-18-22 45-1 19-20-40-34-43 44-31-10-13-4, 33-34-43 22-17-8-12 32-8-34-45 43-35-32-34 36-34-20-23 31-41-8 32-38-22-8-21, 2-27-45-17 42-41-6-13-9-28 40-34-43 20-17-8 8-11-34-16-29-41, 33-34-43 17-8 2-38-42-20-7-3-8-43 41-9-26.

Acts 8:38 SKJV

THE BIBLE'S BOOK OF ACTS: SAUL THE PERSECUTOR BECOMES PAUL THE CHRISTIAN

All at once he saw a light from heaven shining around him. He fell to the ground. Then he heard a voice say, "Saul, Saul, why are you working so hard against Me?"

Acts 9:3-4 NLV

Jewish leaders were afraid of Christianity, Jesus' new church. The book of Acts shows the ultimate persecutor, Saul, who hated Jesus and His followers. But then Saul became a Christian himself after meeting the brightly shining, heavenly Jesus on the road to Damascus! Later called Paul, Saul would join the apostle Peter and other Christian leaders in preaching, working miracles, and strengthening the young church.

95. HOW SAUL WANTED TO HURT THE CHURCH — DECODER

	1	2	3	4	5
1	N	B	I	P	C
2	E	V	R	M	T
3	W	O	F	Q	K
4	A	J	L	Y	H
5	G	X	S	D	U

53-41-55-43 31-41-53 53-25-13-43-43 25-41-43-35-13-11-51 24-55-15-45
41-12-32-55-25 45-32-31 45-21 31-32-55-43-54 43-13-35-21 25-32 35-13-43-43
25-45-21 33-32-43-43-32-31-21-23-53 32-33 25-45-21 43-32-23-54. 45-21
31-21-11-25 25-32 25-45-21 45-21-41-54 23-21-43-13-51-13-32-55-53 43-21-41-54-21-23.
45-21 41-53-35-21-54 33-32-23 43-21-25-25-21-23-53 25-32 12-21 31-23-13-25-25-21-11
25-32 25-45-21 42-21-31-13-53-45 14-43-41-15-21-53 32-33 31-32-23-53-45-13-14
13-11 25-45-21 15-13-25-44 32-33 54-41-24-41-53-15-55-53. 25-45-21 43-21-25-25-21-23-53 31-21-23-21 25-32
53-41-44 25-45-41-25 13-33 45-21 33-32-55-11-54 41-11-44 24-21-11 32-23 31-32-24-21-11 33-32-43-43-32-31-13-11-51
25-45-21 31-41-44 32-33 15-45-23-13-53-25 45-21 24-13-51-45-25 12-23-13-11-51 25-45-21-24 25-32
42-21-23-55-53-41-43-21-24 13-11 15-45-41-13-11-53.

Acts 9:1–2 NLV

96. JESUS CONVERTS SAUL — CROSSWORD

All Quotations NLV

1 2 3 4 5 6 7 8

Across

2 Saul saw a ____ from heaven (Acts 9:3)

5 When Saul got up, he couldn't ____ (Acts 9:8)

6 God said, "This man is the one I have chosen to carry My ____ among the people" (Acts 9:15)

7 After his conversion, Saul stayed on a street called ____ (Acts 9:11)

8 Saul heard the voice of ____ (Acts 9:4–5)

Down

1 Saul was on his way to the city of ____ (Acts 9:3)

3 Saul was blind for ____ days (Acts 9:9)

4 The Lord told ____ about Saul (Acts 9:10–15)

THE BIBLE'S BOOK OF ACTS: PETER LEARNS THAT ANYONE CAN BE SAVED

Then Peter said, "I can see, for sure, that God does not respect one person more than another. He is pleased with any man in any nation who honors Him and does what is right."

Acts 10:34–35 NLV

The book of Acts shows how the Christian faith spread from Jewish people to include Gentiles too. Since the Jews were God's chosen people, some of them struggled to understand how others could be saved as well. Even the apostle Peter needed a special message from God to convince him that all people could be saved!

97. PETER AND THE CENTURION — ACROSTIC

All Quotations SKJV

What was the centurion's name? (Acts 10:1) 30-13-4-22-19-40-25-9-37

An _____ of God came to the centurion in a vision (Acts 10:3) 23-31-16-3-34

What tanner was hosting Peter? (Acts 10:6) 6-35-20-18-39

How many servants did the centurion call? (Acts 10:7) 26-17-5

"Peter went up on the ____" (Acts 10:9) 14-32-2-38-24-10-41-27

The centurion was a ___ man (Acts 10:22) 33-11-28-7

The centurion had gathered his "relatives and close ____" (Acts 10:24) 36-8-15-21-1-29-12

"23-1-29 39-32-17 12-21-31-29 20-24-22 26-41 33-5-27-27-23 23-1-29 30-23-34-40 36-18-8 12-15-20-13-39,

17-14-32-28-3 38-2-4-31-23-20-19 25-6 27-21-7-24-8."

Acts 10:5 SKJV

98. GENTILES ARE SAVED BY JESUS — WORD SEARCH

G N I K A E P S D D
F S W D Y L O H D E
O K H E A R I N G Z
L N N S R J E W S I
L A E I E W Z K S T
O H V R T K O O I P
W T I P E F U R G A
E G G R P N I I D B
R N K U D P F Z Y S
S M C S S T Y L L R

While **Peter** was **speaking**, the Holy **Spirit** came on all who were **hearing** his **words**. The Jewish **followers** who had come along with Peter were **surprised** and wondered because the **gift** of the **Holy** Spirit was also **given** to the people who were not **Jews**. They heard them speak in special **sounds** and give **thanks** to God. Then Peter said, "Will anyone say that these people may not be **baptized**? They have received the Holy Spirit just as we have."

Acts 10:44–47 NLV

THE BIBLE'S BOOK OF ACTS AND THE LETTERS OF PAUL: PAUL SURVIVES A SHIPWRECK

Calling out to those who could swim, he told them to jump into the sea and swim to shore. The others should use wood or anything from the ship. In this way, they all got to shore without getting hurt.

Acts 27:43-44 NLV

The book of Acts is full of exciting stories—many of them about the apostle Paul. Before he became a follower of Jesus, he was called Saul. . .and he tried to destroy the church. But after Jesus saved Paul, he became a great missionary who risked death to share the gospel. On his way to Rome to speak truth to Caesar, the emperor, Paul's ship sank in a storm! But God protected him and all of his shipmates. Paul was one of the most important men in all of Christian history—he even wrote almost half the books of the New Testament!

99. PAUL'S SHIPWRECK—AND GOD'S PROTECTION — WORD SEARCH

Then **Paul stood** up and said to them, "Men, you should have **listened** to me and not left **Crete**. You would not have had this **trouble** and **loss**. But now I want you to **take hope**. No one will **lose** his **life**. Only the **ship** will be lost. I belong to God and I work for Him. Last night an **angel** of God stood by me and said, 'Do not be **afraid**, Paul. You must stand in front of **Caesar**. God has **given** you the lives of all the men on this **ship**.'"
Acts 27:21–24 NLV

L	I	S	T	E	N	E	D	D	S
P	A	N	G	E	L	P	O	N	H
C	L	P	M	K	E	O	T	B	I
K	R	E	K	A	T	P	R	F	P
C	P	E	T	S	L	K	O	L	A
A	L	R	T	O	N	E	U	H	F
E	U	F	S	E	F	E	B	K	R
S	A	S	V	I	C	S	L	X	A
A	P	I	L	R	K	O	E	G	I
R	G	S	H	I	P	L	K	T	D

100. LETTERS OF PAUL — CROSSWORD

All Quotations SKJV

Across

2 Paul's letter to the Colossians says, "Let the ____ of God rule in your hearts" (Colossians 3:15)

5 Paul wrote two letters to this young pastor friend

6 Paul wrote one letter to this young pastor friend

7 Paul's letter that explains the "fruit of the Spirit"

Down

1 Two of Paul's letters to people in this city are in the Bible

2 Paul's shortest letter in the Bible

3 Paul's letter that teaches, "All have sinned and come short of the glory of God"

4 Paul's letter to the Philippians says, "I can do all things through _____ who strengthens me"

THE BIBLE IS ALL ABOUT KNOWING GOD

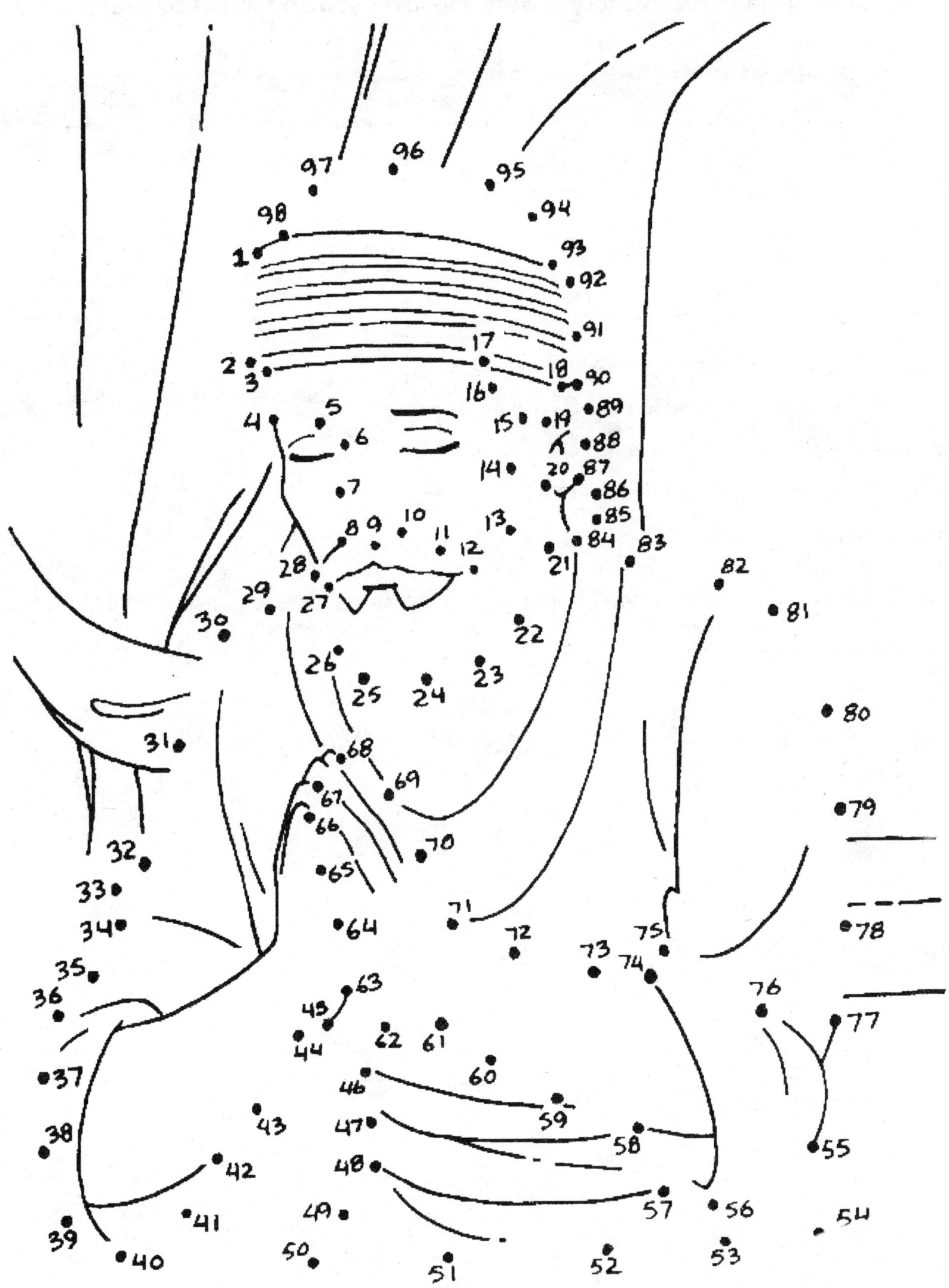

And this I pray, that your love may abound yet more and more in knowledge and in all judgment, that you may approve things that are excellent, that you may be sincere and without offense until the day of Christ, being filled with the fruits of righteousness, which are by Jesus Christ, to the glory and praise of God.

PHILIPPIANS 1:9–11 SKJV

Prayer is just talking with God. You can tell Him you love Him, ask Him for wisdom, or confess your sin to receive forgiveness. He loves you and wants to hear from you!

101. THE LORD'S PRAYER TEACHES US HOW TO PRAY — ACROSTIC

All Quotations SKJV

"Therefore, ____ according to this manner" (Matthew 6:9)	3-18-28-9
"Our ____ ____ is in heaven" (Matthew 6:9)	29-37-10-50-17-48 11-31-23
"Hallowed be ____ ____" (Matthew 6:9)	38-22-51-30 5-36-27-4
"Your ____ come" (Matthew 6:10)	16-40-47-21-49-15-41
"Your will be done on ____ as it is in heaven" (Matthew 6:10)	33-46-2-26-42
"Give us this day our daily ____" (Matthew 6:11)	32-8-43-14-20
"And forgive us our ____, as we forgive our debtors" (Matthew 6:12)	24-45-6-39-12
"And do not ____ us into temptation" (Matthew 6:13)	7-44-19-34
". . .but deliver us from ____" (Matthew 6:13)	25-1-35-13

"29-23-48 9-15-51-8-12 40-12 10-50-17 16-35-5-21-24-23-27 28-47-49 39-42-25 3-22-11-44-2 19-47-49 10-42-45 21-1-15-18-38 29-15-2-43-1-4-30. 46-41-43-5."

MATTHEW 6:13 SKJV

ANSWER KEY

WORD SEARCH

1. Where the Bible Comes from, and What It Does

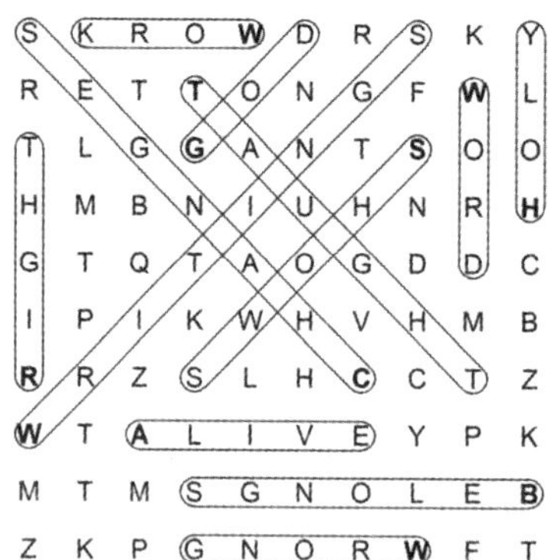

CROSSWORD

2. Names for the Bible, *from* the Bible

DECODER

3. Why We Have the Bible

I have written these things to you who believe in the name of the Son of God, that you may know that you have eternal life, and that you may believe in the name of the Son of God.

1 John 5:13 SKJV

ACROSTIC

4. What the Bible Does

GENESIS / TIMOTHY / JOB / JUDE / PSALMS / SONG OF SOLOMON / REVELATION / MALACHI

For the word of God is living and powerful and sharper than any two-edged sword, piercing even to the dividing of soul and spirit, and of the joints and marrow, and is a discerner of the thoughts and intentions of the heart.

Hebrews 4:12 SKJV

CROSSWORD

5. How the Bible Describes Jesus

WORD SEARCH

6. Who Jesus Is

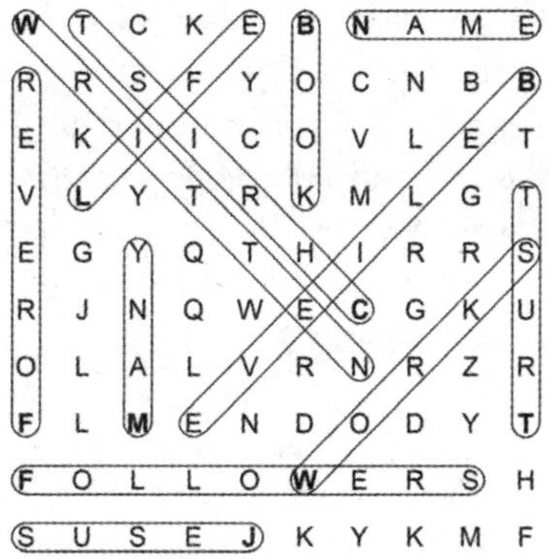

DECODER

7. In the Beginning, God. . .

. . .made from nothing the heavens and the earth. The earth was an empty waste and darkness was over the deep waters. And the Spirit of God was moving over the top of the waters.

Genesis 1:1–2 NLV

CROSSWORD

8. Adam, Eve, and Eden

WORD SEARCH

9. Adam and Eve's Sin

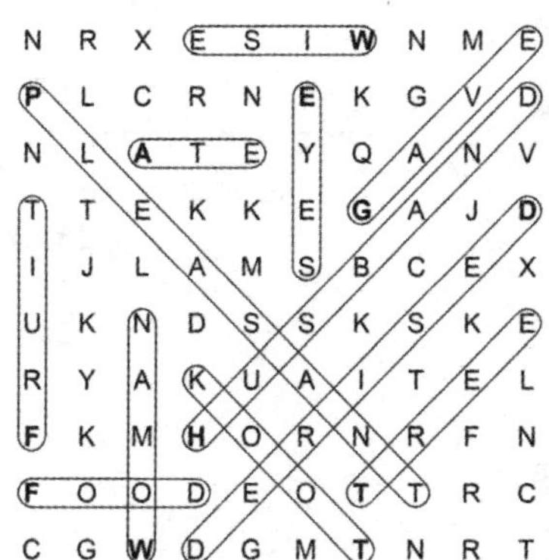

ACROSTIC

10. Cain and Abel

CONCEIVED / MAN / BROTHER / SHEEP / FRUIT / ANGRY / WELL / TALKED

And the Lord said to Cain, "Where is Abel your brother?" And he said, "I do not know. Am I my brother's keeper?" And He said, "What have you done? The voice of your brother's blood cries to Me from the ground."

Genesis 4:9–10 SKJV

CROSSWORD

11. Noah's Ark

				J			S		
				A			O		F
		G	O	P	H	E	R		O
				H			T		R
G	R	A	C	E		F			T
		L		T	H	I	R	T	Y
		T		H		F		H	
		A				T		R	
		R				Y		E	
								E	

DECODER

12. The Rainbow

"When I bring clouds over the earth and the rain-bow is seen in the clouds, I will remember My agreement that is between Me and you and every living thing of all flesh. Never again will the water become a flood to destroy all flesh."

Genesis 9:14–15 NLV

ACROSTIC

13. Abraham and Sarah

WALK / COVENANT / FATHER / ABRAM / LAUGHED / ISAAC

And Abraham called the name of his son who was born to him, whom Sarah bore to him, Isaac.

Genesis 21:3 SKJV

WORD SEARCH

14. Isaac's Twin Sons

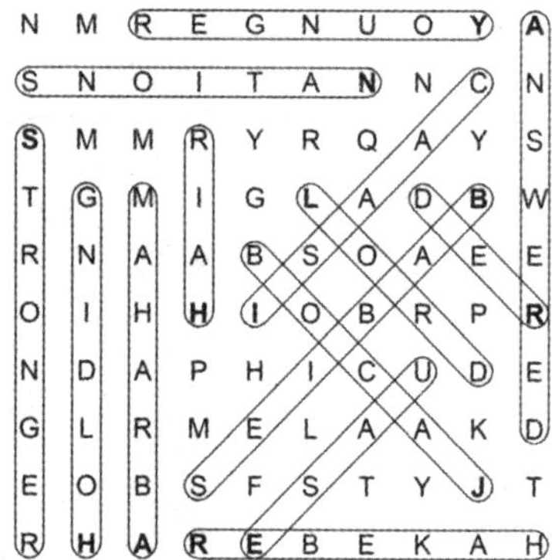

CROSSWORD

15. Young Joseph

DECODER

16. Sold as a Slave!

Some Midianite traders were passing by. So the brothers pulled Joseph up out of the hole. And they sold him to the Ishmaelites for twenty pieces of silver, and they took Joseph to Egypt.

Genesis 37:28 NLV

WORD SEARCH

17. Joseph Explains Pharaoh's Dream

ACROSTIC

18. Joseph Forgives His Brothers

MOURNED / BURY / HATE / FORGIVE / PLACE / SAVE

"But as for you, you thought evil against me, but God meant it for good, to bring to pass, as it is this day, to save many people alive."

GENESIS 50:20 SKJV

CROSSWORD

19. Moses and the Burning Bush

DECODER

20. God Punishes Egypt

The Lord said to Moses. . . "Pharaoh will not listen to you. Then I will lay My hand on Egypt. By great acts that will punish the Egyptians, I will bring out My family groups, My people, the sons of Israel, from the land of Egypt. The Egyptians will know that I am the Lord when I put My hand upon Egypt and bring out the people of Israel from among them."

EXODUS 7:1, 4–5 NLV

WORD SEARCH

21. The Tenth—and Worst—Plague on Egypt

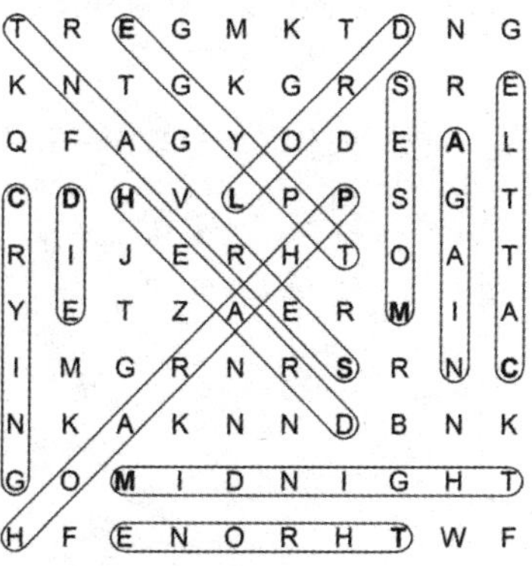

ACROSTIC

22. Parting the Red Sea

STICK / EGYPTIANS / CLOUD / WHEELS / MORNING / AFRAID / BELIEVED

But the people of Israel walked on dry land through the sea. The waters were like a wall to them on their right and on their left.

EXODUS 14:29 NLV

CROSSWORD

23. The Ten Commandments

DECODER

24. Do What God Says!

"Therefore you shall be careful to do as the LORD your God has commanded you. You shall not turn aside to the right hand or to the left."

DEUTERONOMY 5:32 SKJV

ACROSTIC

25. Battle of Jericho

SEVEN / JOSHUA / SPECIAL / BLEW / MORNING / DESTROYED / FELL

The seventh time, when the religious leaders blew their horns, Joshua said to the people, "Call out! For the Lord has given you the city."

JOSHUA 6:16 NLV

WORD SEARCH

26. Joshua's Last Advice for Israel

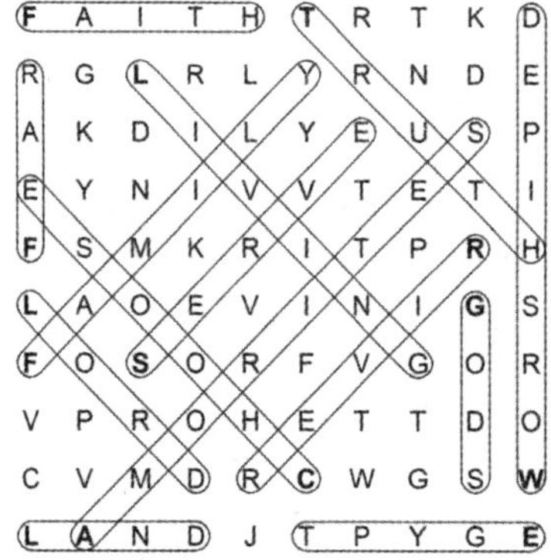

DECODER

27. Judge Deborah Goes into Battle

Now Lappidoth's wife Deborah, a woman who spoke for God, was judging Israel at that time. . . . She sent for Barak. . .and said to him, "The Lord, the God of Israel, says, 'Go to Mount Tabor.'" . . . Barak said to her, "I will go if you go with me. But if you do not go with me, I will not go." And she said, "For sure I will go with you. But the honor will not be yours as you go on your way."

JUDGES 4:4, 6, 8–9 NLV

CROSSWORD

28. Samson's Death

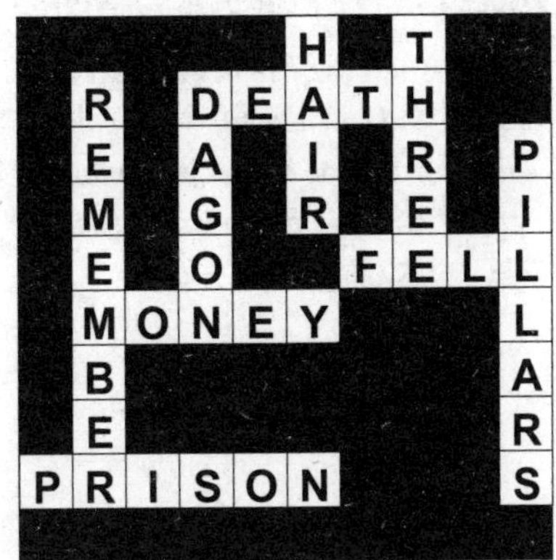

ACROSTIC

29. Ruth and Boaz Meet

BETHLEHEM / YOU / GATHERED / WORK / FAVOR / SPEAKING

So Ruth gathered grain in the field until evening. Then she beat out what she had gathered. It was enough barley to fill a basket.

RUTH 2:17 NLV

WORD SEARCH

30. Ruth and Boaz Start a Family

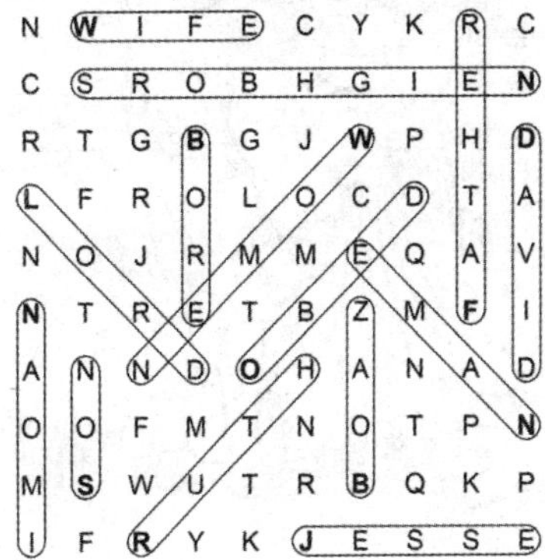

CROSSWORD

31. Samuel and Saul

DECODER

32. Samuel and Saul

And when Samuel saw Saul, the LORD said to him, "Behold the man whom I spoke of to you! This same man shall reign over My people."

1 SAMUEL 9:17 SKJV

ACROSTIC

33. David and His Sling

CHAMPION / CUBITS / GATH / VALLEY / FIVE / BROOK / SWORD

And when the Philistine looked around and saw David, he disdained him, for he was only a youth, and ruddy and had a handsome face.

1 Samuel 17:42 SKJV

WORD SEARCH

34. Jealous King Saul

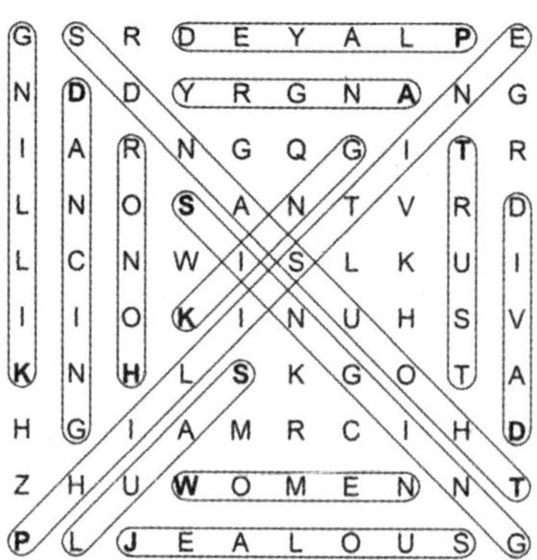

CROSSWORD

35. David and Jonathan

DECODER

36. David Becomes King

And the men of Judah came, and there they anointed David king over the house of Judah. And they told David, saying, "The men of Jabesh-gilead were those who buried Saul." And David sent messengers. . .and said to them, "You are blessed of the LORD that you have shown this kindness to your lord, even to Saul, and have buried him. And now may the LORD show kindness and truth to you."

2 Samuel 2:4–7 SKJV

DECODER

37. Solomon Chooses Wisdom

"Because you have asked this, I have done what you said. See, I have given you a wise and understanding heart. No one has been like you before, and there will be no one like you in the future. I give you what you have not asked, also. I give you both riches and honor. So there will be no king like you all your days. And if you walk in My ways and keep My Laws and Word as your father David did, I will allow you to live a long time."

1 Kings 3:11–14 NLV

WORD SEARCH

38. Israel Splits in Two

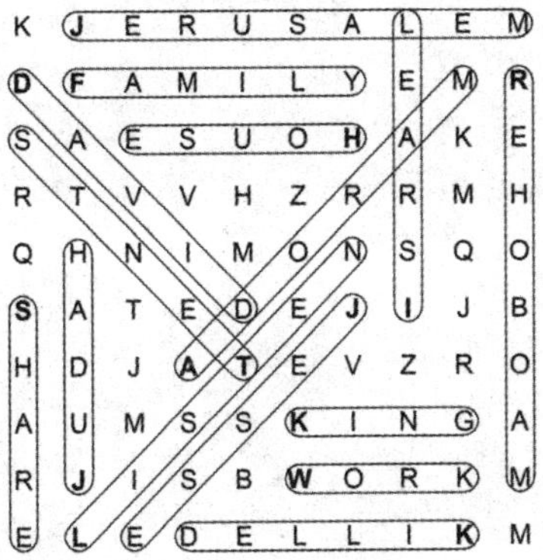

CROSSWORD

39. Elijah and the False Prophets

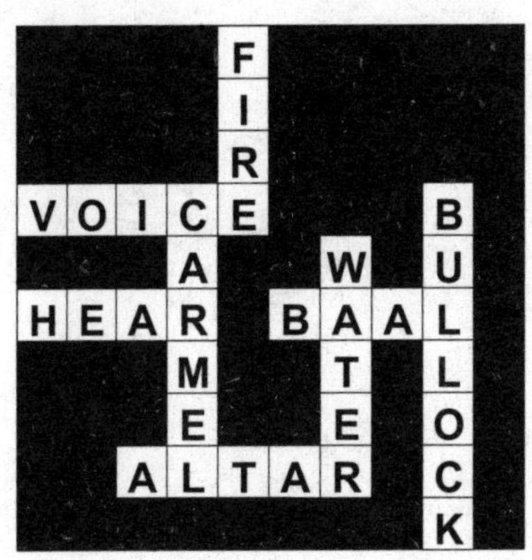

DECODER

40. Elijah Goes to Heaven Without Dying!

And it came to pass, as they still went on, and talked, that, behold, there appeared a chariot of fire, and horses of fire, and parted them both asunder; and Elijah went up by a whirlwind into heaven. And Elisha saw it, and he cried, My father, my father, the chariot of Israel, and the horsemen thereof.

2 Kings 2:11–12 KJV

WORD SEARCH

41. Josiah, the Boy King

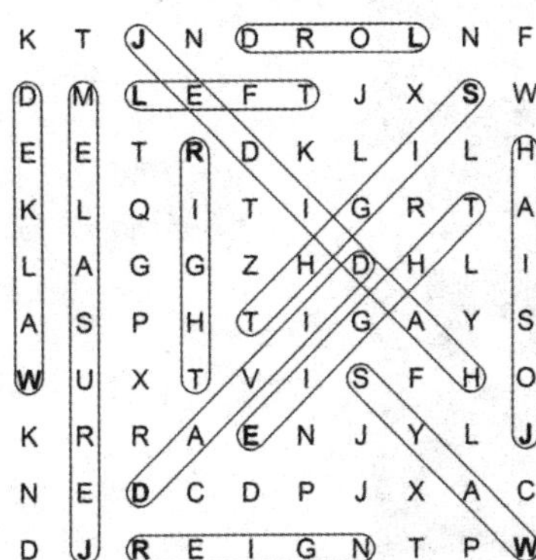

DECODER

42. God Finally Punishes His People for Their Sin

Then the king of Assyria carried the people of Israel away against their will to Assyria. . . . Because the people of Israel did not obey the voice of the Lord their God. They sinned against His agreement and even all that the Lord's servant Moses told them. They would not listen or obey.

2 Kings 18:11–12 NLV

CROSSWORD

43. Nehemiah in Jerusalem

WORD SEARCH

44. Examples of the Work

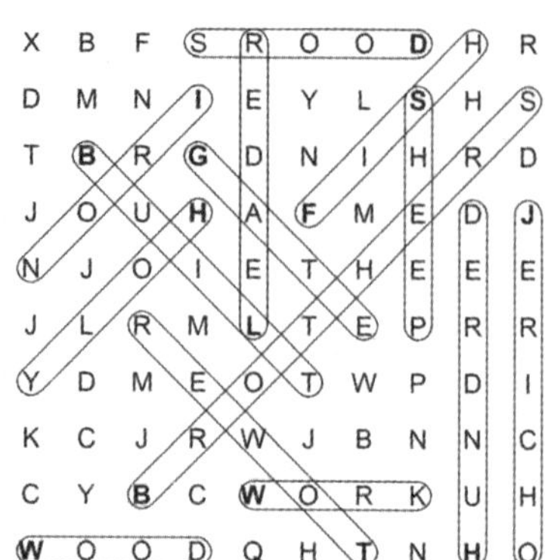

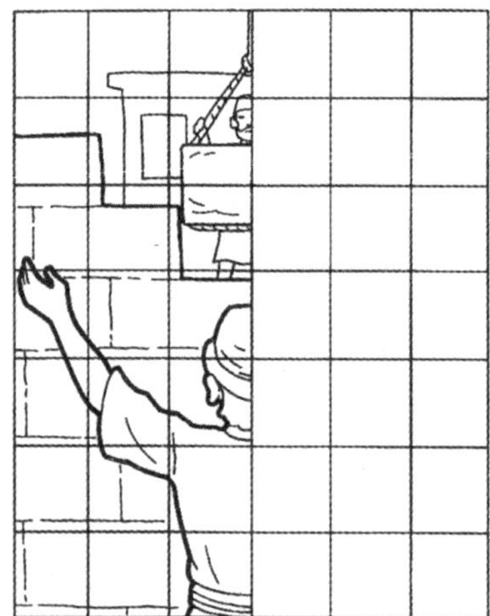

WORD SEARCH

45. Workers and Fighters

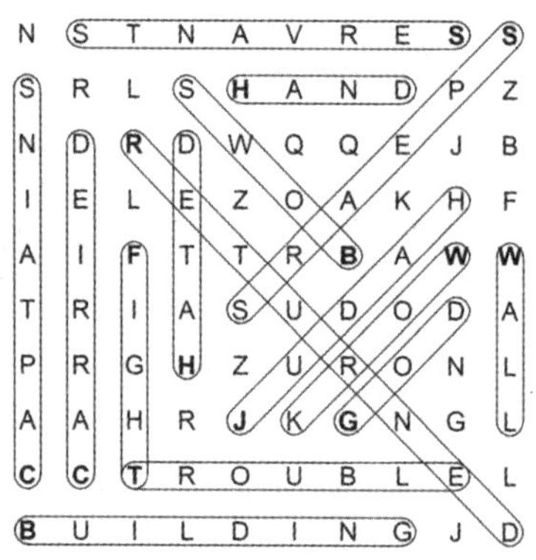

ACROSTIC

46. Success!

JERUSALEM / FOUNTAIN / WATER / TOBIAH / AFRAID / JOY

So the wall was finished on the twenty-fifth day of the month of Elul, in fifty-two days.

NEHEMIAH 6:15 SKJV

CROSSWORD

47. Queen Esther

DECODER

48. The Woman for the Hour

"For if you keep quiet at this time, help will come to the Jews from another place. But you and your father's house will be destroyed. Who knows if you have not become queen for such a time as this?"

ESTHER 4:14 NLV

ACROSTIC

49. The Fiery Furnace

FOUR / WORSHIP / ANGRY / CLOTHES / SMELL / LAND

The three men were still tied up when they fell into the fire.

DANIEL 3:23 NLV

WORD SEARCH

50. God Shows Nebuchadnezzar Who's Boss

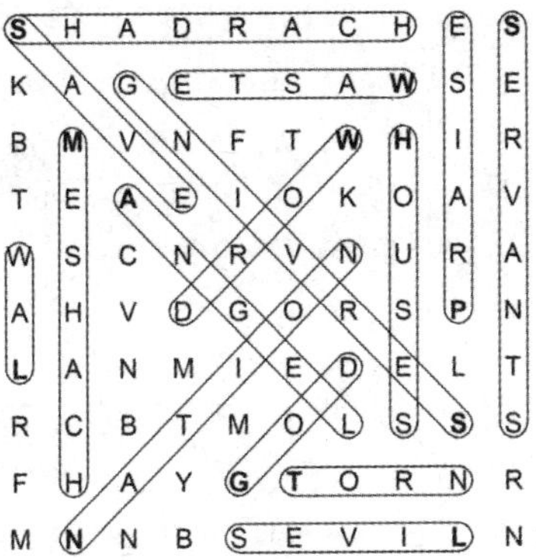

CROSSWORD

51. Daniel and the Lions

DECODER

52. Daniel's Vision of the End Times

"I saw in the night visions and, behold, one like the Son of Man came with the clouds of heaven and came to the Ancient of Days, and they brought Him near before Him. And dominion and glory and a kingdom were given to Him, that all people, nations, and languages should serve Him."

DANIEL 7:13–14 SKJV

ACROSTIC

53. Jonah Overboard

NINEVEH / JOPPA / NAMES / COUNTRY / FEAR / BLOWING / STOPPED

The Lord sent a big fish to swallow Jonah, and he was in the stomach of the fish for three days and three nights.

JONAH 1:17 NLV

WORD SEARCH

54. Jonah Should Have Cared More for Nineveh

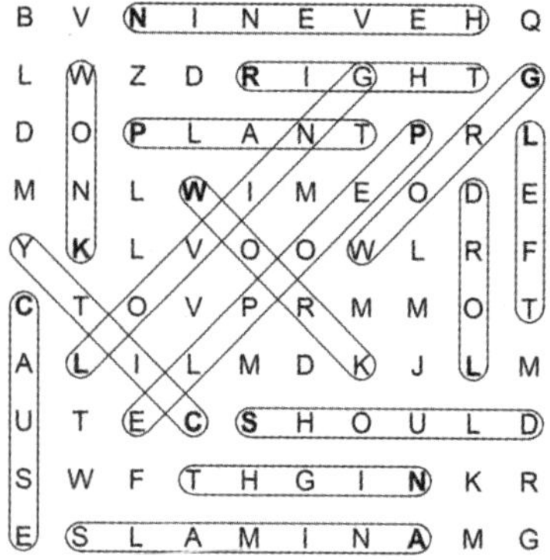

CROSSWORD

55. God Sends an Angel to Visit Mary

DECODER

56. Mary Is Expecting a Very Special Baby

The birth of Jesus Christ was like this: Mary His mother had been promised in marriage to Joseph. Before they were married, it was learned that she was to have a baby by the Holy Spirit. Joseph. . .thought it would be good to break the promised marriage without people knowing it. While he was thinking about this, an angel of the Lord came to him in a dream. The angel said, "Joseph, son of David, do not be afraid to take Mary as your wife."

MATTHEW 1:18–20 NLV

ACROSTIC

57. Mary, Joseph, and Baby Jesus

BETHLEHEM / DAVID / SWADDLING / MANGER / FLOCK / SUDDENLY

"For to you is born this day in the city of David a Savior, who is Christ the Lord."

LUKE 2:11 SKJV

WORD SEARCH

58. The Very First Christmas

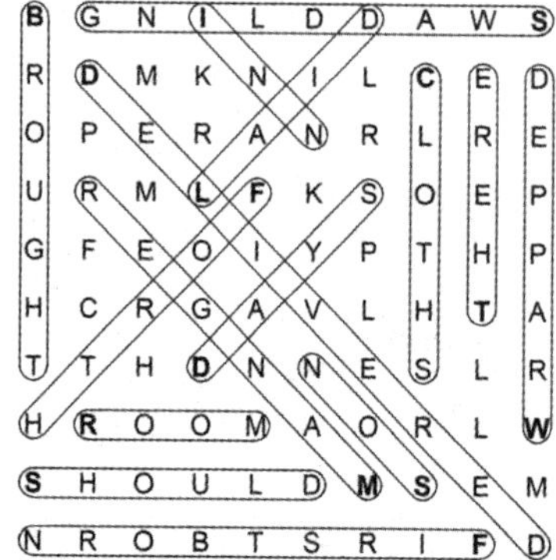

CROSSWORD

59. Christmas Shepherds

DECODER

60. Shepherds Share the Good News

And they came with haste and found Mary and Joseph, and the baby lying in a manger. And when they had seen it, they widely made known the saying that was told them concerning this Child.

LUKE 2:16–17 SKJV

WORD SEARCH

61. The Visit of the Wise Men

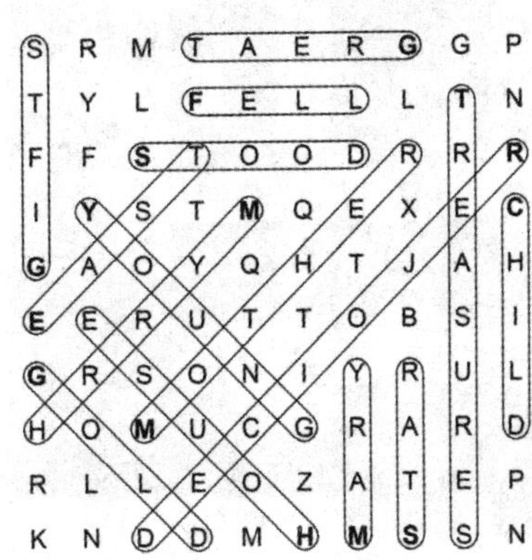

DECODER

62. Young Jesus in the Temple

And when He was twelve years old, they went up to Jerusalem according to the custom of the feast. . . . And it came to pass that after three days they found Him in the temple, sitting in the midst of the teachers, both hearing them and asking them questions. And all who heard Him were astonished at His understanding and answers.

LUKE 2:42, 46–47 SKJV

CROSSWORD

63. John Baptizes Jesus

DECODER

64. How John the Baptist Described Jesus

The next day John the Baptist saw Jesus coming to him. He said, "See! The Lamb of God Who takes away the sin of the world! I have been talking about Him. I said, 'One is coming after me Who is more important than I, because He lived before I was born.' I did not know who He was, but I have come to baptize with water so the Jews might know about Him."

JOHN 1:29–31 NLV

ACROSTIC

65. Jesus Is Tempted in the Wilderness

FORTY / BREAD / LIVE / JERUSALEM / TEMPT / WORSHIP

Jesus was led by the Holy Spirit to a desert. There He was tempted by the devil.

MATTHEW 4:1 NLV

WORD SEARCH

66. Jesus Calls His First Disciples

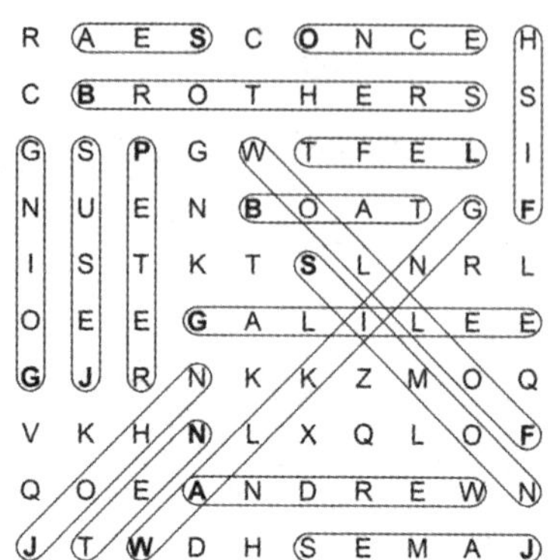

CROSSWORD

67. Jesus' First Miracle

ACROSTIC

68. Jesus in the Temple

JEWS / JERUSALEM / CHANGING / WHIP / MONEY / TURNED / FATHER'S / BUYING

Then His followers remembered that it was written in the Holy Writings, "I am jealous for the honor of Your house."

JOHN 2:17 NLV

WORD SEARCH

69. Jesus and Woman at the Well

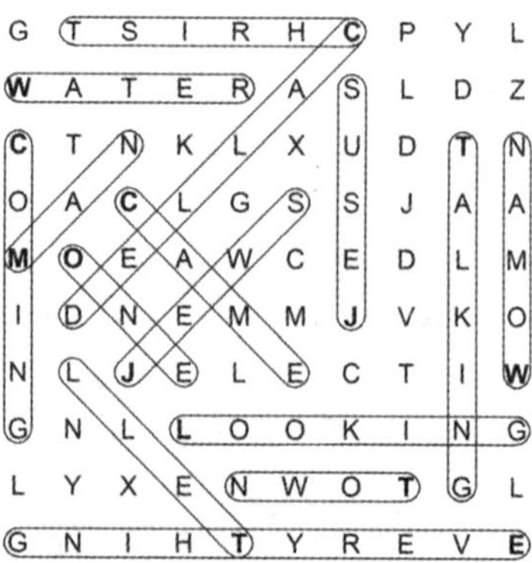

DECODER

70. Samaritans Follow Jesus

Many people in that town of Samaria. . .said to the woman, "Now we believe! It is no longer because of what you said about Jesus but we have heard Him ourselves. We know, for sure, that He is the Christ, the One Who saves men of this world from the punishment of their sins."

JOHN 4:39, 42 NLV

WORD SEARCH

71. Jesus and the Leper

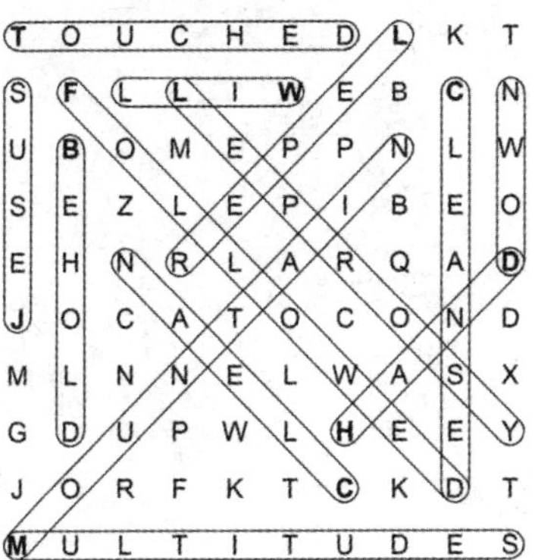

CROSSWORD

72. Jesus and the Centurion

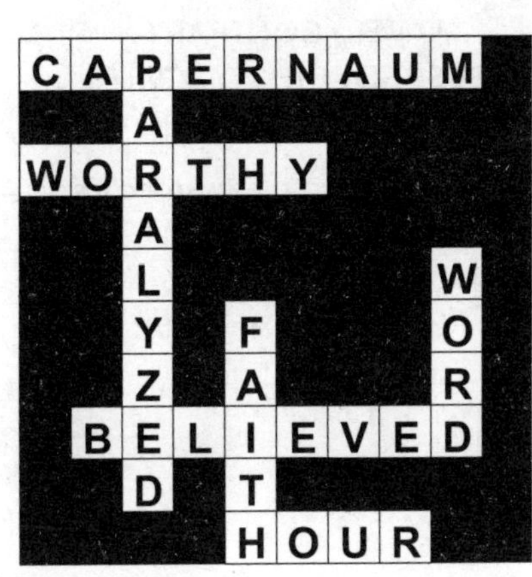

ACROSTIC

73. Jesus Calms the Stormy Sea

EVENING / BOAT / STORM / TEACHER / WORDS / QUIET / WHY / FAITH

They were very much afraid and said to each other, "Who is this? Even the wind and waves obey Him!"

MARK 4:41 NLV

WORD SEARCH

74. Jesus Heals a Demon-Possessed Man

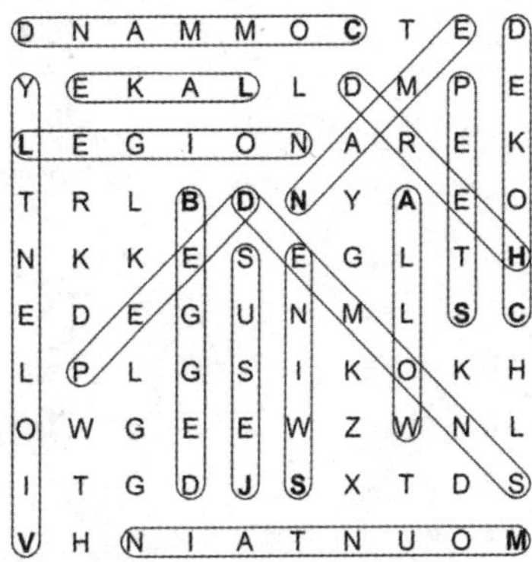

CROSSWORD

75. The Bread and the Fish

DECODER

76. Peter Understands Who Jesus Is

While Jesus was praying alone, His followers were with Him. Jesus asked them, "Who do people say that I am?" They said, "John the Baptist, but some say Elijah. Others say that one of the early preachers has been raised from the dead." Jesus said to them, "But who do you say that I am?" Peter said, "You are the Christ of God."

Luke 9:18–20 NLV

ACROSTIC

77. Peter Sinks in the Sea

WAVES / CONTRARY / JESUS / FOURTH / DISCIPLES / COME / BEGINNING

And immediately Jesus stretched out His hand and caught him, and said to him, "O you of little faith, why did you doubt?"

Matthew 14:31 SKJV

WORD SEARCH

78. "Truly You Are the Son of God"

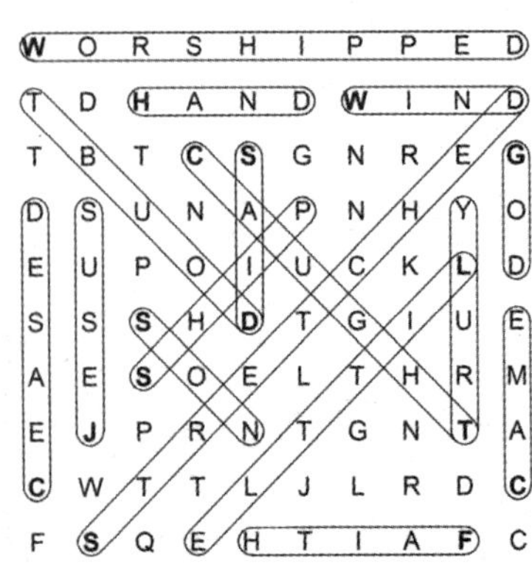

DECODER

79. The Transfiguration

About eight days after Jesus had said these things, He took Peter and James and John with Him. They went up on a mountain to pray. As Jesus prayed, He was changed in looks before them. His clothes became white and shining bright.

Luke 9:28–29 NLV

WORD SEARCH

80. Jesus, Moses, and Elijah

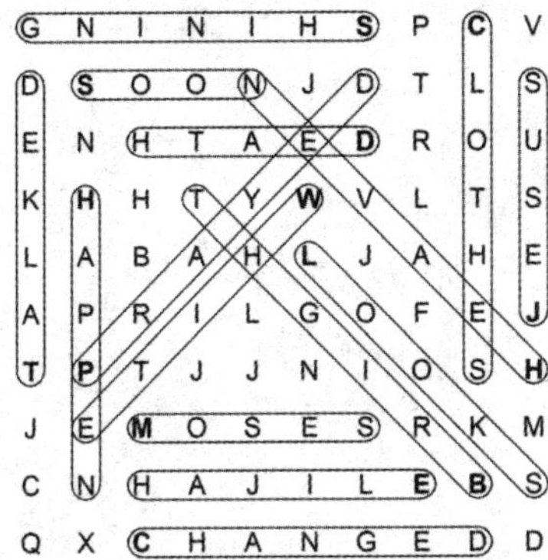

ACROSTIC

81. Jesus and the Children

CHILDREN / REBUKED / DISPLEASED / LITTLE / KINGDOM

And He took them up in His arms, put His hands on them, and blessed them.

MARK 10:16 SKJV

WORD SEARCH

82. Receive the Kingdom of God Like a Little Child

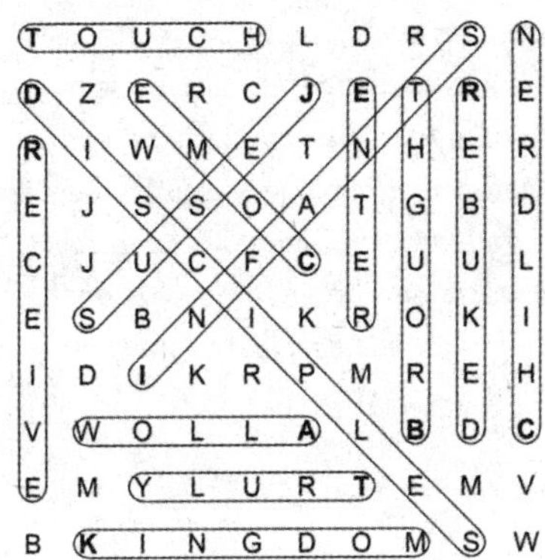

CROSSWORD

83. The Triumphal Entry

DECODER

84. Jesus the Prophet from Nazareth

And when He had come into Jerusalem, all the city was moved, saying, "Who is this?" And the multitude said, "This is Jesus the prophet from Nazareth of Galilee."

MATTHEW 21:10–11 SKJV

ACROSTIC

85. Jesus Betrayed

ISCARIOT / RELIGIOUS / SILVER / JESUS / TWELVE / HAND / LORD / MY

Judas was the one who was handing Jesus over. He said, "Teacher, am I the one?" Jesus said to him, "You have said it."

MATTHEW 26:25 NLV

WORD SEARCH

86. Judas' Sad Ending

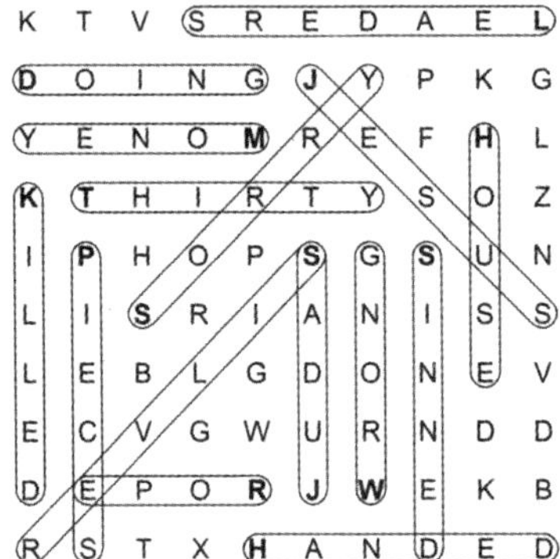

CROSSWORD

87. Jesus on the Cross

DECODER

88. Jesus Is Buried

Then they took the body of Jesus with the spices and put it in linen cloths. This was the way the Jews made a body ready for the grave. There was a garden near the place where He had been nailed to the cross. In the garden there was a new grave in the side of the hill. No one had ever been laid there.

JOHN 19:40–41 NLV

ACROSTIC

89. After the Resurrection

HAVE / CHRIST / FATHER / BETHANY / BLESSED / WORSHIPPED / JERUSALEM

And it came to pass, while He blessed them, He was parted from them and was carried up into heaven.

LUKE 24:51 SKJV

WORD SEARCH

90. Jesus' Ascension

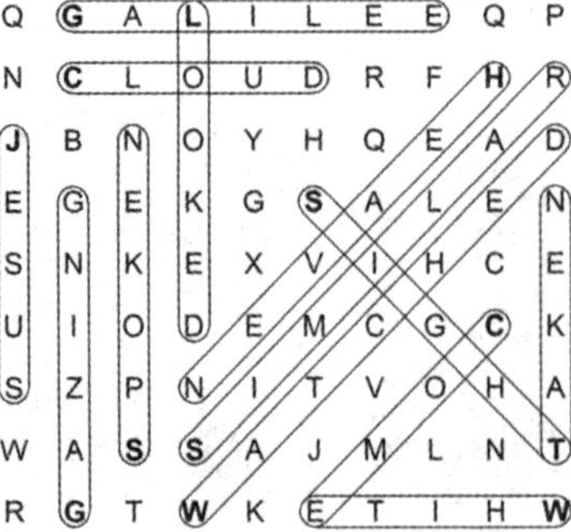

CROSSWORD

91. The Day of Pentecost

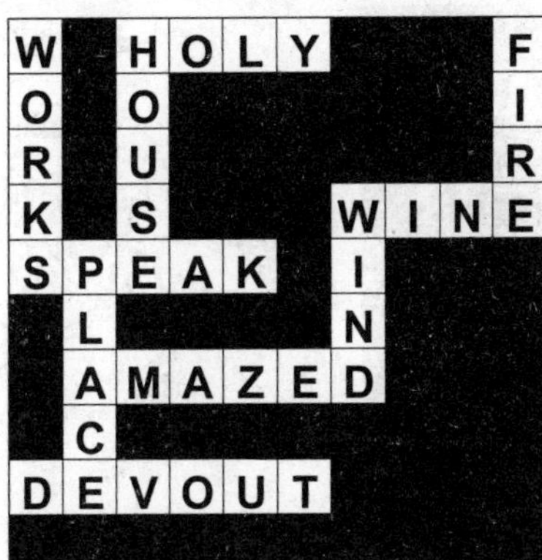

WORD SEARCH

92. What Really Happened at Pentecost

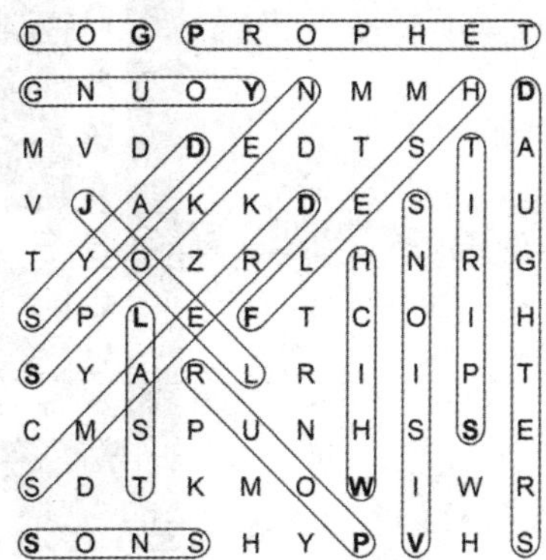

WORD SEARCH

93. Christians Scatter and Share Jesus

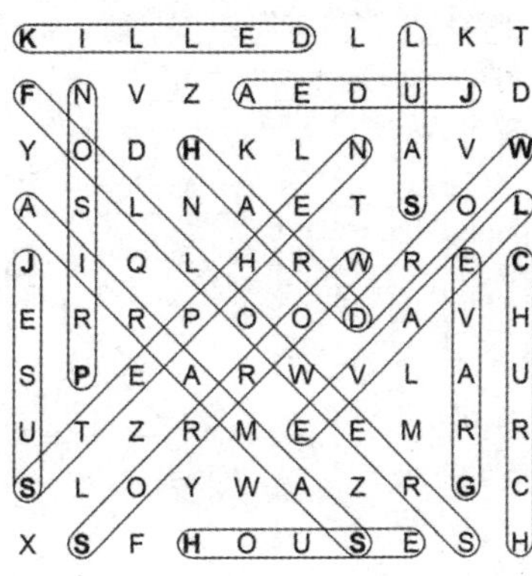

ACROSTIC

94. Philip and the Ethiopian Eunuch

LORD / AUTHORITY / WORSHIP / SPIRIT / LAMB / REJOICING / AZOTUS

And he commanded the chariot to stand still, and they went down into the water, both Philip and the eunuch, and he baptized him.

Acts 8:38 SKJV

DECODER

95. How Saul Wanted to Hurt the Church

Saul was still talking much about how he would like to kill the followers of the Lord. He went to the head religious leader. He asked for letters to be written to the Jewish places of worship in the city of Damascus. The letters were to say that if he found any men or women following the Way of Christ he might bring them to Jerusalem in chains.

Acts 9:1–2 NLV

CROSSWORD

96. Jesus Converts Saul

ACROSTIC

97. Peter and the Centurion

CORNELIUS / ANGEL / SIMON / TWO / HOUSETOP / JUST / FRIENDS

"And now send men to Joppa and call for Simon, whose surname is Peter."
Acts 10:5 SKJV

WORD SEARCH

98. Gentiles Are Saved by Jesus

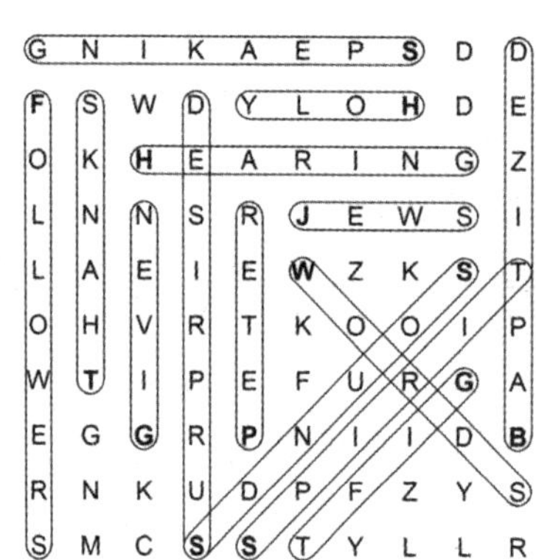

WORD SEARCH

99. Paul's Shipwreck—and God's Protection

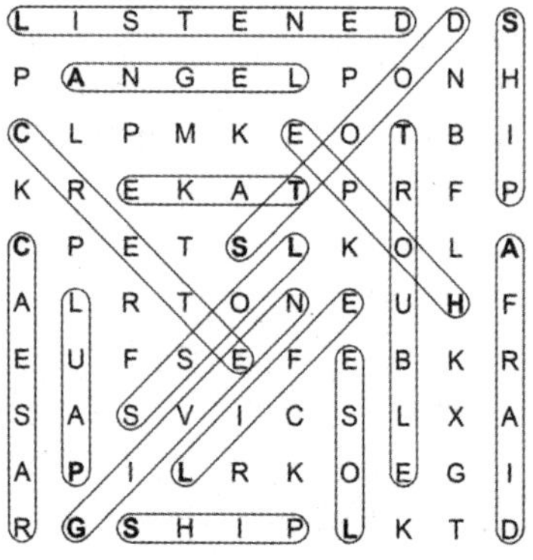

CROSSWORD

100. Letters of Paul

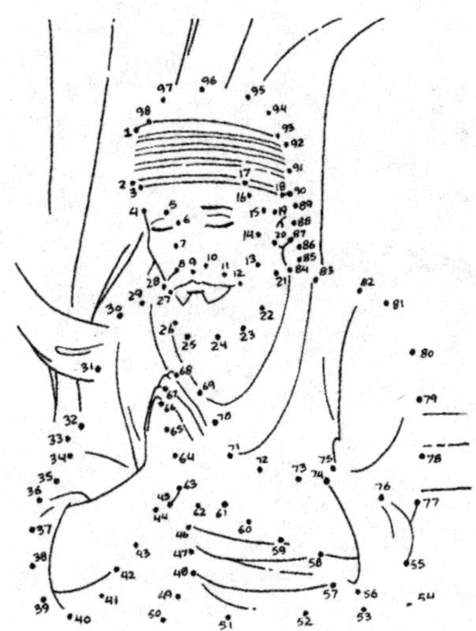

ACROSTIC

101. The Lord's Prayer Teaches Us How to Pray

PRAY / FATHER WHO /
YOUR NAME / KINGDOM /
EARTH / BREAD / DEBTS /
LEAD / EVIL

"For Yours is the kingdom and the power and the glory forever. Amen."

MATTHEW 6:13 SKJV

MORE GREAT BIBLE FUN!

Perfect for 6-to-10-year-olds, *Phones Down Bible Activity Fun* promises hours of scripture-based entertainment and education. With over 100 activities—including crosswords, word searches, secret codes, fill-in-the-blanks, and picture fun pages—this book covers the entire Bible, from Genesis to Revelation.

Paperback / ISBN 979-8-89151-144-6

Find This and More from Barbour Books at Your Favorite Bookstore or www.barbourbooks.com